The Affirmation of Life

The Affirmation of Life

A Reichian Energetic Perspective

by
John Lawson

Ardengrove Press
Portland, Oregon

The Affirmation of Life

Ardengrove Press
P.O. Box 219014
Portland, Oregon 97225

Library of Congress Catalog Card Number: 91-075 113

ISBN 0-9630338-1-6

Publisher's Cataloging Data (Library of Congress CIP data unavailable for this edition)

1. Personal growth   2. Body-mind connection
3. Reichian Energetics   4. Title (Psychology)

For ordering information, please see page 126.

For Elaine

and Shelley

Contents

Contents

IV Body, Mind, and Spirit

To the Reader

How we feel about life - the value that life holds for us - is a direct expression of how we function as human beings. This means that if we wish to change our attitude toward life, we must change our functioning. Doing so involves a practical task.

The present book is offered in the hope of providing some understanding of the challenge of developing and maintaining an affirmative attitude toward life in the context of the modern world. The discussion is rooted in issues arising in the course of my practice as a private instructor in Reichian Energetics. The latter is a form of personal growth work based on the bio-energetic principles and techniques introduced by Wilhelm Reich.

Most of the material included in these pages has been published previously, either privately, or in the journal, *Transformation Times*. I have reorganized the contents and made some revisions.

I hope that the reader will find value in the presentation that follows. It represents an attempt to see and understand a variety of human problems from a functional, energetic standpoint.

John Lawson
Portland, Oregon

I.

The Affirmation of Life

Many painters are afraid of the blank
canvas, but the blank canvas is afraid of
the real passionate painter who dares.

Vincent Van Gogh

The Affirmation of Life

We live in a world in which it is difficult to maintain an affirmative attitude toward life. I believe this statement is true, and I believe most serious people would agree with it. In a sense, the present discussion is a testimony to the difficulties and challenges that we all face in the contemporary world. It is only when the value and meaning of existence have become in some degree problematical that we seek to establish a deeper basis for our commitment to life and a firmer practical foundation for our personal growth.

Reichian Energetics is a form of personal growth work based on the holistic principles formulated and advanced by the late Wilhelm Reich. The focus of this type of work - which takes place in individual sessions of private instruction - is on improved health and personal functioning. I am not a medical doctor, nor does the work I do involve the diagnosis or treatment of specific pathology. Nonetheless, I am interested in promoting health, and that means the overall vigor, vitality, and well-being of the individual. In the process of seeking to bring about improved functioning, I find that - in a deep sense - our capacity for health is a reflection of our capacity for life. If we can understand the impediments that obstruct optimal functioning, then we have a chance to dissolve them and to use the liberated energy for our personal growth. To do this, however, involves a challenging task. Why this task is challenging will, I hope, become apparent in the course of the present discussion.

What are some of the obstacles that serve to obstruct healthy functioning? Clearly, there are many possible responses to this question. On the medical level, there are the various types of specific pathology which medical doctors are trained to diagnose and treat. Sociologically, there are the stresses and strains of a particular set of relationships that form the basic matrix of interpersonal communication in the contemporary world. Culturally, there are the ideas, the ideals, and the imperatives in terms of which adjustment to society is presently mandated. All of us must contend at some time or another with infection, competition, and disappointment. These are an unavoidable part of modern living. We may take issue with the injustice of these often gratuitous encounters, yet in the world in which we live they are unavoidable.

Reichian Energetics is a form of practice that takes into account the various obstacles to improved functioning with which each of us must contend. In this work, we try to be aware realistically of the way the world is, just as we also take into consideration our feelings about the way it should be. I believe that some of the original insights of Wilhelm Reich are especially relevant to understanding how to confront and work through on a personal level some of the resistance points to more satisfying functioning.

As some of you may know, Reich was an associate of Sigmund Freud for a number of years. Then, in the early 1930's, he went his own way. Reich disagreed with Freud on a number of issues. Especially, he contested the assumption that human beings are characterized biologically by a "death instinct." Freud had suggested, in his book *Beyond the Pleasure Principle*, that there were two opposing forces in each human being. One was a drive for life and pleasure, reflected most clearly in the striving for sexual love and meaningful work. The other biological tendency, Freud maintained, was toward the resolution of tension that comes with death. This tendency, according to Freud, represented an instinctual urge to return to an inanimate state of being, free from pain.

14

Reich, however, saw things differently. He could not deny - based on his experience with his clients and his observations of the world around him - that there were, indeed, powerful, death-oriented, destructive forces in operation. At the same time - based again on his contact with his clients and his extensive observation of himself and others - he was convinced that at the deepest level of human experience the force of life is primary. According to Reich, only when the positive impulse of life becomes frustrated and hampered in a fundamental way does it then reappear in an altered, secondary form as an inclination toward death and destruction.

In order to put into focus some of the concrete implications of Reich's thinking, let's pause for a moment. Let's move from the 1930's to the present. Let's take this opportunity to observe ourselves. The area I want to call to your attention is breathing. Observe for an instant how you are breathing. Is your jaw loose, or is it tight? Notice whether your chest is participating in your respiration. Is your chest rising and falling as you breathe? What about your diaphragm? What about your abdomen? Can you feel any sensation of movement in your pelvis as you exhale? Do you feel a connection between your vision and the rhythm of your breathing? And do you feel your feet on the floor? If I were to be poetic, I might ask: do you feel connected to the ground as you breathe? These questions are not extraneous. They are the kinds of questions that Wilhelm Reich came to ask in the context of his work with individual clients. These questions are significant in relation to our overall functioning.

You will remember that we said that Reich was in disagreement with Freud about the issue of a death instinct. In fact, Reich ceased to practice psychoanalysis. Instead, he proceeded to work with his clients in terms of their overall functioning. This focus has been carried over into the practice of Reichian Energetics. Basically, there are three main aspects to the Reichian Energetic approach:

[1] *Breathing* is systematically expanded and deepened in order to *mobilize increased energy and feeling.*

[2] *Chronic muscular tension is dissolved* according to a well defined set of procedures that are tailored specifically to individual needs.

[3] *At the verbal level,* the experience of change and increased awareness is drawn into a meaningful focus and *grounded* through discussion.

How does this tie in with the challenge of maintaining an affirmative attitude toward life in the modern world, and how does it relate to the subject of Reich's disagreement with Freud?

In his work with clients, Reich came to view the average person in terms of a specific organization of the body structure and a definite pattern of energetic functioning. This is one of the reasons why, a few moments ago, I asked you to stop for a minute and focus attention on your involuntary processes. Each one of us is breathing, and each one of us has assumed a more or less characteristic posture. Our posture is evident in our appearance and behavior, and it is also sensed directly by us as "who we are." Our posture is intimately related to our breathing, and together the two reflect the level of our energetic functioning. Another term which conveys the same dynamics that I am describing here with the word "posture" is the term "character structure." That term was employed by Reich. One of his outstanding books is entitled *Character Analysis.*

At this point, let's pause again for a moment. This time, of course, be aware of your breathing. You might even want to take a deep breath now, simply to renew your energies. Also, however, focus attention on your shoulders. You are probably sitting in a chair. Are your shoulders relaxed? Do you feel any strain in your neck? Is there any uncomfortable tension at the base of your skull? Can you feel your shoulders as a kind of "easy yoke," as a balancing point in a comfortable, upright posture? Is your pelvis relaxed? Is it a true "basin" - which is what the word "pelvis" means? The pelvis contains our sexual organs and is an important factor in postural balance.

In Reichian Energetics, we work with the breathing process to deepen, expand, and facilitate more adequate respiration. We also work to reduce or eliminate patterns of chronic muscular tension, which Wilhelm Reich referred to as "armor." The effect of this process, when successfully carried through, is to provide the opportunity for a more or less thorough "housecleaning" with respect to longstanding restrictions in structure and function. The precise details of this approach provide the subject for a separate discussion. What I want to focus on now is that what emerges from this style of work is an awareness that the attitude of each person is related to the function and structure of that same person. I will illustrate with an example.

A person who - for whatever reason - chronically contracts the musculature around the eyes will have difficulty seeing things clearly. Included in the set of muscles to which I am referring are the frontal, temporal, parietal, and occipital groups of muscles, as well as the smaller muscles either directly attached to or immediately in the neighborhood of the eyeballs. What I am saying is that the degree of chronic spasticity or "tightness" in this region affects ones vision. I am using the word "vision" here to mean more than just the mechanical process of refracting images. I am talking about vision in the deeper sense of "insight." As a prefatory quotation in one of his books, Reich cites Goethe:

> What is the hardest thing of all?
> That which seems the easiest:
> For your eyes to see
> That which lies before your eyes.

Another example of the way in which personal structure and function are related to our attitude toward life is the heart. We are so familiar with the heart as a pump, and with the vital role that this pump plays, that we may forget that the heart is also a center of feeling. The heart is a very strong organ, yet in our culture and time this organ is subjected to a great deal of insult and injury. To protect our heart, most of us in one way or another adopt a posture which will afford us the greatest possible insulation from pain and disappointment. In doing so, we may for the time being protect our heart, but we also isolate ourselves from the joy, as well as the risks, of a more heartfelt existence. One of Wilhelm Reich's former students, Alexander Lowen, has investigated this area. Some of you may be familiar with Lowen's approach, called Bioenergetic Analysis.

The eyes and the heart are important organs by means of which we make contact with life, and their use as examples here is intended to raise a question. How is it possible to maintain a deeply felt, affirmative attitude toward life if our experience of life is habitually restricted? I have said that our function and structure are related to our attitude toward life. Now I would go one step further. I believe that, strictly speaking, our function and structure *are* our attitude toward life.

Another example that I could give of the functional identity of our basic posture and our attitude toward life would be our legs and feet. In many respects, our feet are neglected parts of our bodies these days. Shoes - especially those designed for women - do not really seem to be made to walk in. But defects in styles of footwear are secondary to the earlier stresses and strains to which our legs and feet are subjected. Frequently, for example, there is pressure on young children to walk before they are ready. Such performance allows the parent to view the child as special. Oftentimes a child will be reprimanded for falling, or the parent will not offer support and assistance when the child is in need. At other times the parent may be overly protective. In any of these cases, self-support and healthy contact with the earth are made difficult. We speak of a person capable of taking a stand as "rooted in reality." Such a person, in a literal way, can "understand" his or her situation and has the ability to "stand up to life."

Not only our posture, but our breathing as well is a key factor in our attitude toward life. Most people know that breathing can be sheer hell for the person suffering from asthma or emphysema. What many people do not know is that breathing that is not "clinically" deficient can still be sufficiently inadequate to turn life into a state of limbo. One of the important links between respiration and the functioning of the person as a whole is the role of breathing in energy regulation. The combustion processes of our metabolism have been compared by Alexander Lowen to the combustion that takes place in a wood burning fire. Both processes require sufficient oxygen for the flame to be a strong one. The finest fuel will not burn if there is inadequate oxygen. Breathing is directly linked to energy levels in all of us.

Given these considerations, I think it may be clear why I have said that it is difficult for most people to maintain an affirmative attitude toward life in today's world. It is difficult to maintain such an attitude, because a really affirmative approach to life can only be based on a deeply felt identification with the healthy functioning of ones own life processes. This means a relatively unhampered capacity to breathe deeply, to feel, and to move. Unfortunately, such capacities are not commonly found among human beings today. In fact, they appear to be quite rare. Precisely for that reason I would consider that an affirmative attitude toward life is a challenge. In saying this, I do not feel pessimistic.

All difficulties that we wish to overcome or work through present a challenge. If the difficulties were not relevant to our desires and needs, we would not view them as obstacles to our growth and development. Then we could ignore them, and there would be no price to pay for our ignorance. But ignoring obstacles that are truly in the way of our health and well-being can be destructive, both of ourselves and others. Confronting challenges, therefore, is a necessary part of the process of living.

An affirmative attitude toward life does not mean that "all is for the best in this best of all possible worlds." Voltaire satirized this attitude in his classic novel, *Candide.* An affirmative attitude toward life is a challenge because it is difficult. The difficulties that we face are many. We live in a world in which social pressures are extreme, and excessive competition is pervasive. Simply to disregard these pressures does not help, since this leaves us open to needless injury and unhappiness. Our prevailing culture, to which we are all vulnerable to one extent or another, makes demands on us which are not only difficult or impossible to fulfill, but which are contradictory and therefore confusing. In addition to these pressures, we live in a world in which there is much violence, with a threat of greater violence still to come. Under these conditions, we may ask, is it realistic to affirm the value of life?

With respect to that question, each one of us has to arrive at his or her own conclusion, and certainly there are times when each of us may feel despair. It is helpful, however, to keep in mind some important distinctions. Life is not synonymous with the culture in which we live. Life is not the same as any given social order. And life is not identical to any specific moment of history. If we take an affirmative stance toward life, we need not affirm or support unreservedly any given context in which life unfolds.

What then, we may ask again, is life? That question cannot be answered analytically, and we will, therefore, search in vain throughout textbooks of biology for a satisfactory definition. This may seem surprising, since the word "biology" means "science of life." Nonetheless, it is true. Fortunately, however, every individual is to some extent in touch with the feeling of being alive, and it is on the basis of our shared experience of being alive that we dare to talk about "life." This brings us back to the question of the nature and value of being alive, a question which in practice each one of us must confront daily.

If Wilhelm Reich was correct, then life is basically an expressive, pulsatory process which functions in terms of the gratification of fundamental needs. In this process, each one of us strives for fulfillment. If this is the case, then in practice the question we face is: what can we do to confront and work through the obstacles that stand in the way of a more gratifying existence?

The nature of this challenge is met in Reichian Energetics by confronting the obstacles in our habitual way of doing things. Our habits develop over a more or less substantial period of time, and they become quite firmly ingrained in our image of ourselves. The earlier a habit is established, the more deeply entrenched it becomes. The range of our movements and the scope of our experience become set in innumerable ways. The whole constellation of our habitual patterns takes on a familiar quality. Even though our posture may cause us distress, and our breathing and energy may be dampened, we become accustomed to "being the way we are." Nonetheless, frequently we desire change. This creates a dilemma. As Moshe Feldenkrais has stated in his book, *The Potent Self,* "paradoxical as it may seem, people do want to change themselves and to remain at the same time what they are."

As I have indicated, the process of Reichian Energetics involves a challenging approach. If we wish to deepen, expand, and improve our functioning, we must confront the limitations structured into our habitual experience and behavior. Fortunately, learning to confront and work through the restrictions in our respiration and learning to reduce chronic muscular tension can help significantly to broaden the range of our responses. This means, literally, an increase in personal "responsibility." Changes of this kind are related to a rise in the energy level of the person and an opening up of avenues for energetic discharge in meaningful activity and more committed living. This, in turn, becomes possible only as one learns to establish and maintain a more balanced posture and "stance in life."

It can be seen, I think, that Reichian Energetics involves a learning process. In this, it is similar in certain respects to some other approaches that focus on the interrelation of human structure and function. In my view the Reichian Energetic approach has various strong points, one of which is the major focus on breathing and energy. Another is the detailed understanding of the relationship between postural attitude and personal history. Still, I should emphasize that this approach is not a panacea. To make such an assumption would not be realistic.

In my remarks so far, I have placed considerable emphasis on what some people may consider "negative" issues. For example, I have made no secret of the fact that I think that life can be tough. I have suggested that maintaining an affirmative attitude toward life is not always easy. I have spoken in terms of challenge rather than in terms of success. This has been necessary in order to examine seriously some important questions. Nonetheless, it is my firm conviction that life is a powerful force that becomes all the more worth living as we gain the courage to confront the obstacles that stand in the way of our improved health and functioning.

Let us now examine in more detail some of the obstacles, issues, and possibilities that are related to our personal growth. Since we all come into the world as newborn babies, we will begin our discussion by taking a look at some of the early stages in our development as individuals and the manner in which these stages are reflected in the expressive language of our bodies.

II.

First Principles

The happiness and well-being of children depend on the degree of love and approval we give them.

A.S. Neill

Early Stages in Personal Growth

Among the living species so far discovered, humans are the least subject to fixed biological patterns. This view is borne out by the diversity of cultural and social arrangements recorded in history. The very flexibility and malleability of human beings form the basis for complex personal and social growth.

At the same time that we recognize the wide range of differences in experience and behavior that separate individual human beings from one another, we must also remember that beneath the surface of our individuality all of us are alike in basic respects. Another way of saying this is to emphasize that there are certain common functioning principles which are at the root of all human action and experience. One such basic principle that governs the life of our species - as well as all other known forms of life - is the inborn tendency which we have to move *toward* pleasure and *away* from pain. The spontaneous action of shrinking in the face of pain is known as anxiety. Generally, we can say that living organisms *expand* with pleasure and *contract* in anxiety. Insight into this basic living process is at the core of Freud's formulation of the "pleasure principle." Simply stated, this principle asserts that human beings seek to repeat experiences of pleasure and to avoid pain. If we keep in view the fundamental, biological nature of the role of pleasure and pain in life, we need not see human action in relativistic terms. Our experience and behavior may be relative to our particular situation, but the intelligibility of our experience and behavior is rooted in the biological depths of our human nature. This is significant with respect to the early development of each one of us.

Affirmation of Life

It has become increasingly clear that in the life of each person the intrauterine environment, in which we originally grow and develop, has a profound and lasting effect upon us. In bio-energetic terms, the basic issue is whether the mother is generally relaxed and free of excessive anxiety during pregnancy, or whether the womb is tight and constricted. To appreciate this matter, we must remember that all of us have spent approximately the first nine months of our existence in the womb of a woman. As R.D. Laing has emphasized, it makes a difference which womb has been our first home. If we were to have the opportunity to be conceived again, Laing asks, in the body of what woman would we choose to grow? What would the criteria for our selection be? Thinking along these lines, it is not so difficult to see that the degree of healthy biological functioning in the baby prior to birth is intimately related to the openness, acceptance, and pulsation of the mother's organism.

The experience of birth itself - as Frederick Leboyer points out in his book, *Birth Without Violence* - may be either traumatic or reassuring, depending on various factors. The ability of the mother to surrender and give into the spontaneous waves of expansion and contraction during labor is important. The birth process *per se* engages mother and child in an intense energetic pulsation - the "contractions" of labor - culminating in the emergence into the world of a new creature.

Upon being born, the new infant comes immediately into functional contact with its surroundings. The bio-energetic aliveness of the expressions of the mother, the father, and other humans present is of great importance. This is true with respect to eye contact, for the newborn will be responsive to deep, sincere expressions of emotion communicated through the eyes of those who share the birth experience. Equally

28

important are the warmth and sensitivity of skin contact and the knowing, secure, and loving support given in holding and attending to the baby. Again, to appreciate these matters, let us simply ask the question: How would I like to be received into the world if I were being born? (We may wish also to ask the question: How *was* I received into the world when I *was* born?)

During the period immediately following birth and for the first few years of life, breast milk is not only a natural form of nourishment for the child, but the act of nursing provides necessary gratification in sucking and deep pleasure through intimate contact with the mother - visually, tangibly, energetically, and emotionally. The ability to reach out and take in pleasure from the environment is learned in a fundamental way at this early stage. To use Karen Horney's expression, a feeling of "basic security" is established through the experience of closeness to the mother.

After birth, the first three or four years of life are a period of rapid personal development marked by the consolidation of a variety of capabilities on the part of the child. Locomotion, control of the eliminative functions, and weaning are all naturally established during this period. From approximately the age of four years, the swing of the energy movement of the person is toward the continuing integration of the various bodily and personality functions, culminating in the securing of the young child's identity as an autonomous being, conscious in a positive way of his or her sexuality, and capable of deep, intelligent self-expression.

In our contemporary environment it is unusual to find young children in whom the natural stages of early growth have occurred without interruption or hindrance. This is important. Serious restrictions in the growth process necessarily become embodied personally in patterns of inhibited respiration, chronic muscular tension, and depressed or otherwise disturbed energy levels. Such interruptions in the early stages of growth, perpetuated and reinforced as they typically are in subsequent stages, are important factors serving to limit self-expression and restrict the exercise of a more meaningful range of human options.

Fortunately, however, much valuable knowledge and information are now available to assist in the learning of new approaches to establishing conditions for healthier growth during the early stages of life. Many insights into the processes of vital human development along the lines of bio-energetic principles have been gained. Natural childbirth practices, renewed interest in extended breastfeeding, and serious questioning of the goals and methods of child education are significant. In addition, personal growth work based on a sound functional approach can help to alleviate the stresses that are related to problems that have already taken shape in the course of our individual development.

There are many factors that human beings must take into consideration when making decisions, and there is much in life that is precarious and unknown. We act, hopefully, in our own best interest. Long before we act consciously to achieve specific goals, however, we are already engaged in a process of self-education and personal development based on our striving to satisfy our fundamental needs. It is those needs and the process of their gratification that are the underlying basis for our growth from the earliest stages of life to adulthood.

To arrive at such a view may appear to leave us in a somewhat nebulous position when confronted with the task of attempting to understand the manner in which an individual's personal history has influenced his or her present-day experience and behavior. How are we to arrive at more than fanciful judgments concerning such an issue? The answer to this question is to be found in the shape and mold of a person's physical structure. The concrete history of our growth is revealed, for each of us, in the form and movement of our bodies, which are the vehicles of our self-expression.

Self-Expression and the Body

It was the great French novelist, Stendhal, who suggested that man invented speech in order to conceal his thoughts. While spoken language can be one of the central tools which human beings use as a valid means of self-expression, Stendhal's point was well-taken. Words can easily be employed successfully as a means of avoidance or subterfuge. The same cannot be said, however, of the language of the body. Any habitual posture that restricts the free-flowing vitality of the organism will represent clearly the restricted quality of experience of that same organism. It is this essential feature of the body as a faithful conveyor of experience that serves as one of the key reference points in the functional energetic approach to personal growth.

In his book, *Character Analysis,* Wilhelm Reich took the fundamental first steps toward presenting an integrated, systematic understanding of the relationship between mind and body. It was Reich's contention that at the deep level of organismic processes, mind and body are *functionally identical.* According to this view, the body is not merely a physico-chemical complex reducible, ultimately, to the laws of inorganic matter. Rather, it is understood and sensed to be the expression of energetic processes fundamental and specific to living nature. As such, in its structure and function, the body is the expression of who we are.

To say that the body is a direct expression of who we are is to suggest that, in life, experience and behavior are functionally identical. All of our behavior - whether it be the forcefulness of our handshake or the rhythmicity of our heartbeat - reveals the texture of our subjective world. By the same token, our experience is the subjective rendering of the movements of our organism, both at the voluntary and the vegetative level. In the deep sense, what is at issue are the energetic processes of life itself. Such a situation can be represented by means of the following diagram, which was introduced by Reich.

Body 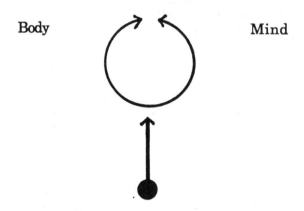 Mind

Bio-energetic Processes

Based on his understanding of the underlying unity of mind and body, Reich succeeded in delineating a practical method for promoting improved individual functioning. According to Reich's reasoning, the identity of *psyche* and *soma,* at the level of bio-energetic processes, provides the basis for expanding and deepening the practice of personal growth work beyond the sphere of verbal analysis, on the one hand, and behavior modification, on the other. The common ground where experience and behavior meet is the living body. In effect, for Reich, the goal of improved individual functioning increasingly came to be associated with freeing the organism from patterns of chronic muscular tension, which he referred to as a form of "armor." This involved especially the consistent dissolution of blocks in the respiratory process, resulting in a substantially increased energy level.

Reich's integrated viewpoint comprehended the fact that experience, in the form of free-flowing contact with oneself and the world, entails the absence of major functional impediments in bodily motility (Figs. 1, 2). In practical work based upon Reich's insights, therefore, careful attention must be paid to the quality of breathing, the range of movement, the muscular tonus, and the verbal communication of each client. This adds feasibility to the attempt to promote the improved functioning of the individual as a whole.

Understanding the body to be the living expression of the person provides an opportunity to overcome those deep splits which characterize not only the individual existence of many persons, but which define and delimit our prevailing cultural and social framework. The primary such split which currently holds sway is the disjunction between thought and feeling. Because we are feeling and thinking individuals by nature, Reich's view indicates that merely thinking about life does not provide the *experience* of life. To gain that experience, one must go beneath the surface phenomenon of words to the depth of bodily awareness, in the interest of which legitimate speech is always initiated.

It is important to understand that thought and feeling can only be joined together constructively when the underlying integrity of the body is established on a

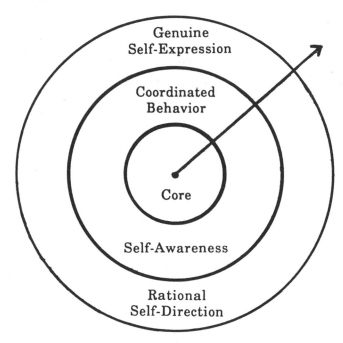

Figure #1: Integrated Self-Expression

Unimpeded flow of energy from the biological core of the organism is expressed in the coordinated behavior of the person. The individual's connection to the environment is secure, and the movement of impulses is direct. Breathing is deep. Energy is full.

Loss of Contact:
Interaction with
Environment Fragmented

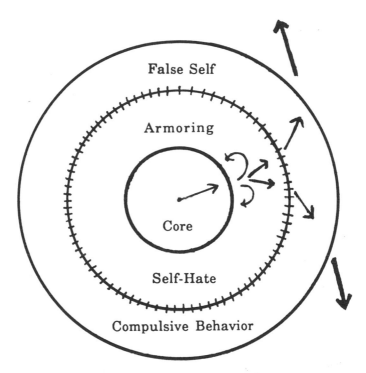

Figure #2: Disturbed Self-Expression

Flow of energy from the biological core is impeded by armoring. Some impulses turn back against the self; others go off at a tangent. Contact with self and environment is split. Energy is bound up in chronic muscular tensions. Breathing is restricted.

firm foundation. This is a task well worth the effort, since integrating personal functioning at the level of the living body offers the rewards of enhanced contact with reality and deepened pleasure in being alive. This condition, in turn, creates the necessary basis for genuine self-esteem.

Based on our awareness of the importance of the early stages in our personal growth, and with an understanding that the structure and function of our bodies reveal in accurate ways the history of our individual experience, we are now in a position to consider a variety of specific issues and problems that affect our capacity to establish and maintain an affirmative attitude toward life.

III.

Problems and Possibilities

The world is quite interesting when you learn to
influence it ever so little.

Moshe Feldenkrais

The Bio-Energetic Basis of Self-Esteem

In the language of contemporary psychology, as well as in everyday usage, "self-esteem" is a term frequently employed to refer to the estimate we make regarding our self-worth. Because a lack of genuine self-esteem is inevitably associated with a degree of discomfort and pain, it is understandable that various attempts have been made to outline ways to promote an improved sense of self. Exercises in assertiveness training, repetition of phrases of self-affirmation, the reinforcement of a positive self-image through the use of recorded tapes, the employment of self-hypnosis, and the pursuit of positive thinking are among several methods that have been suggested. Genuine self-esteem, however, has its roots in levels of our personality that run much deeper than the messages we convey to ourselves on a controlled or premeditated basis. It is out of the depth of our experience of life and the bio-energetic functions which constitute our nature that we ultimately learn to estimate our self-worth.

To say that our self-esteem is based upon bio-energetic principles is to draw a distinction between what is primary and what is secondary in our nature. Few people would deny that long before we begin to think in any complicated fashion, we have the capacity for feeling. The baby who cries in its cradle expresses its discomfort, and even though it cannot yet speak to communicate its distress, it reaches out to us with its cries. The feeling parent will respond by attending to the infant in a caring way. If the parent is successful, the infant will cease crying and begin to make happy sounds or fall back into a contented sleep. The appeal of the infant through crying is not a calculated attempt to solicit aid. Rather, it is a direct expression, bio-energetically, of its state of being at the time, just as an involuntary smile is the expression of the baby's spontaneous opening up to pleasure. Such deep and fundamental expressive functions are examples of our primary nature as living creatures and human beings.

It is because we are sentient beings in our deepest nature that we can appreciate the importance of bio-energetic principles as constituting the essential basis for evaluating our self-worth. While we may need to look at ourselves more positively and view ourselves with increased compassion and understanding, the ability to do so in an authentically constructive manner will depend significantly on the degree to which our capacity for pleasure, feeling, and energetic aliveness remains open. The individual who is fundamentally open and capable of a wide range of movement and expression will experience and put into action a harmonious balance of thought, movement, feeling, and sensation. Such a balance, typified by a relatively graceful alignment of the segments of the body and an adequate energy level, is the natural foundation for self-esteem (Fig. 3). For such an individual, the opinion one has about oneself derives from the good feeling one has in being a person. This good feeling, in turn, is expressed in the goals, activities, and positive struggles of life.

While it is important to be aware of the qualities which characterize genuine self-esteem, we must acknowledge that the stresses of contemporary living pose significant challenges to our mental and physical resources - the very stuff of who we are. These resources are the product of our gradual development from dependent, almost exclusively feeling, newborn babies to rational, decision-making adults. In the course of our growth, leading up to and continuing throughout adulthood, the extent to which the necessary satisfaction of our primary needs is thwarted will determine the degree to which we will sense a lack of

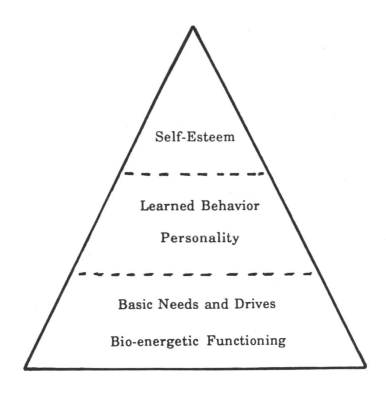

Figure #3: Genuine Self-Esteem

Genuine self-esteem is rooted in the depth of bio-energetic functions. Such self-esteem represents the free flow of energy moving through the person. This movement is registered in consciousness.

fulfillment manifested in diminished self-esteem. This lack of self-esteem will be reflected not only in our mental attitude about ourselves, but in the structure and function of our bodies. Thus, in an individual whose self-esteem is low, we may expect to find a characteristically diminished level of energy associated with restrictions in the breathing process, along with patterns of chronic muscular tension. The exact imbalances in the person's structure will depend on the specific history of the individual and on the compensatory postures that have been devised to create a secondary self-image that is intended to conceal a deep sense of insecurity and self-hatred (Fig. 4).

It may be suspected that the relatively widespread emphasis today on the importance of self-esteem is related to a general lack of it in contemporary living. In place of genuine self-esteem, we are much more likely to encounter the phenomenon of narcissism, which results from investing ones energies in the cultivation of an unreal image. This cultivation of a false self-image is intended to provide a solution. In fact, it creates a serious problem.

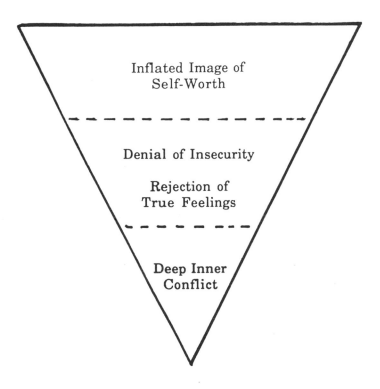

Inflated Image of
Self-Worth

Denial of Insecurity

Rejection of
True Feelings

Deep Inner
Conflict

Figure #4: Inflated Self-Esteem

An inflated self-image rests on an insecure basis, like a triangle standing on its apex. A person cut off from the depths of bio-energetic processes must inflate his or her self-image, drawing energy up into the head. This displacement of energy serves as a defense against underlying insecurities.

The Problem of Narcissism

In Greek mythology, Narcissus was a handsome youth who fell in love with his own image reflected in a pool of water, and thereafter he wasted away due to unsatisfied desire. The term "narcissist," broadly speaking, refers to an individual who is enslaved by an image of himself and who is out of touch with his true feelings. The narcissistic man or woman strives to actualize a glorified self-image which, in reality, is a mask hiding an inner sense of loss, hurt, and desperation.

In his book, *Narcissism: Denial of the True Self,* Alexander Lowen provides an analysis of the predisposing factors leading to the development of narcissism. It is Lowen's argument that on a social level narcissism develops as a response to cultural pressures, while on an individual level it is a response to the crippling stresses of a conflict-torn family situation. Lowen identifies overstimulation and emotional seduction of the child by the parents - especially the parent of the opposite sex - as crucial factors provoking the formation of narcissistic traits in personality.

One of the points emphasized by Lowen in his book is that the basic cultural orientation of the modern world has undergone a drastic turnabout in the course of the twentieth century. This is most evident with respect to sexual mores, which not so terribly long ago were ruled by strict Victorian standards. Such standards denigrated sexuality as beastly and beneath the dignity of human beings, while love was seen as a spiritual affair, a matter of the soul. Today, however, sexual prudery has given way to sexual sophistication, exhibitionism, and pornography. Individuals are able to change sexual partners almost as easily as they switch

44

channels on a television set. Lowen's point is that there has been a basic shift not only in our cultural world, but in our personal world as well. That world - embodied in our personality and including our sexuality - has become less oriented toward feeling and more oriented toward success and power.

We live in a world in which images play a seductive role. By striving to actualize these images rather than our true selves, we deny our deeper needs and feelings. Underneath this striving is to be found the still present horror of an unresolved childhood situation in which there was "too much, too soon." The bargain made by the narcissist is Faustian in nature, for it involves exchanging ones soul for ephemeral and superficial rewards. The price is the loss of ones real self. Such a one-sided contract can only be understood in terms of the helplessness of the child who must respond to the seductive demands of adults or else face the terror of abandonment.

In the context of a narcissistic culture, it is to the genuine advantage of each individual to gain an increased understanding of the conflicts - both social and personal - which make the narcissistic bargain attractive. By so doing, we make it easier to focus our primary attention in the direction of our true feelings and desires, which is the realm where our potential for growth and pleasure is to be found. At a deep level, this means learning to distinguish between the seductiveness of an alluring image and the abiding reality of bodily experience.

The Image and the Body

Anyone who chooses to direct attention to the messages conveyed by the advertising media in the context of present cultural circumstances will quickly discover that much emphasis is placed on the human body. A little thought, however, will soon lead one to conclude that the human body is not so much the real focus of concern as might at first have been supposed. Rather, it is the *image* of the body that has become the preoccupation of many individuals. The body has become, to a considerable extent, a kind of currency that may be used for purchasing a career, a mate, or a friend. The style of a particular hairdo or the contours of a specific human physique are portrayed as the symbols of success. As with all such symbols which are cultivated, there is a widespread recourse to guiding images. In the present social environment, these images are often purveyed by professional artists, actors, and models, as well as by celebrities in general. The tragedy of such a situation is that the images which are projected in the popular media are often destructive of the basic values of a healthy body. In order to provide a basis for the critical evaluation of the seductive messages which are so rampant in our culture, it is helpful to draw a distinction between the image of the body and the reality of the body.

We live in a cultural milieu that is beguiled by images. One of the problems with images is that they lack substance. Very often in discussions with individuals, I become aware that someone seems to be extremely attached to an image of what is presumed to be the only real way to exist as a person. Such an image represents an ideal, and failure to live up to a given ideal is seen as an unacceptable failure (Fig. 5). Thus, a person may struggle relentlessly to achieve an ideal while sacrificing the possibility of genuine pleasure. I sometimes illustrate this dilemma by pointing out that the most beautiful photograph of the most wonderful meal is of no value at all, nutritionally, compared to a real hamburger, even if the hamburger is simple fare by gourmet standards. If one accepts the plain reality of a situation, it may be possible to work toward improving the substance of ones life. The image of a beautiful meal, however, will never satisfy ones actual hunger.

An interesting comment on the pervasiveness of destructive images in our contemporary world has been provided by the movie actor, Kirk Douglas. In an article published in the August, 1987, issue of *Parade* magazine, Douglas recounts a conversation which he had with John Wayne concerning the movie, *Lust for Life,* in which Douglas portrayed Vincent Van Gogh. In John Wayne's opinion, Douglas should not have acted the part of the sensitive artist. "Tough guys like us have an obligation to keep that image for the audience," Wayne insisted. "Come on," Douglas replied. "It's all make believe." Wayne, however, could not be convinced. In Douglas' words: "He really thought he *was* John Wayne."

In the life of the person, the image of the body must be distinguished from the underlying *experience* of the body. It is the experience of the body which is the basis of the image. If image and experience are in harmony, then an individual will be at home in his or her bodily sensations, and his or her self-awareness will be basically free of distortion (Fig. 6) While such harmony is rare in our culture, it is not an impossibility. One of the requisites for moving in the direction of improved psycho-physical balance is to adopt a critical attitude toward the seductive poses which are disseminated so prolifically in the communications media.

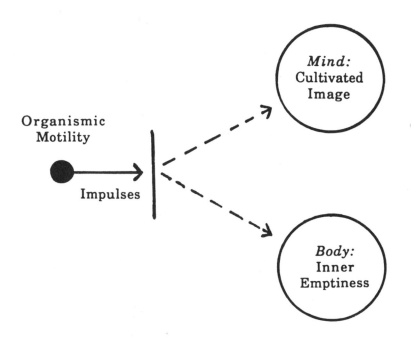

Figure #5: Mind-Body Split

When the natural flow of feeling is blocked due to armoring, the experience of the body is split into a cultivated public image, or "front," and a hidden, private experience of emptiness.

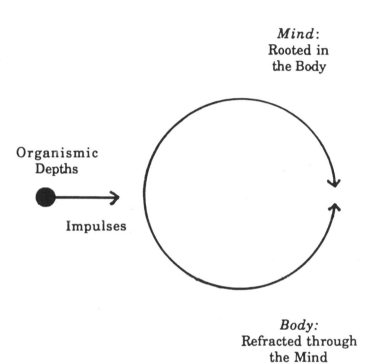

Figure #6: Mind-Body Integration

When the movement of biological energy is unimpeded, mind and body are unified as complementary aspects of a functional whole. Image and sensation are anchored in the bio-energetic depths of the organism.

Leaving aside for the moment the packaging and selling of sexual imagery, perhaps the most immediately recognizable image of health and fitness that is commonly projected today involves the image of being slender. What is striking about so many advertisements recommending loss of weight in connection with a particular food product is that the models in these ads often appear to be emaciated. Of course, different eras embody different attitudes concerning the nature of beauty. Reubens or Renoir would find the contemporary emphasis on being thin incomprehensible. Perhaps such an image is related to the idea that being skinny reflects a high energy level which can tolerate no build-up of fat. The models who appear in such ads, however, often look starved. To recognize this fact is not meant to endorse a condition of being overweight. It is to suggest that the image one projects and with which one identifies on a bodily level may serve to mask an underlying reality which is itself very different from the projected image.

If the true basis of a healthy image of the body is the underlying experience of the deep somatic processes of the person, how then can one arrive at any *objective* orientation in talking about such matters? In terms of the framework proposed by Wilhelm Reich, the answer to that question is to be found in the lively quality of our bodily expressiveness. There are several objectively discernible characteristics of a lively state of being. Among them are deep and unrestricted respiration, an absence of major patterns of chronic muscular tension in the body, and a general openness and responsiveness at the level of the functional processes of the person reflected in good skin tone, brightness of the eyes, and a well organized balance of the physical segments of the body. When unhampered by armoring, the various aspects of personal functioning are experienced as pleasurable, and they are expressed in behavior which is graceful and poised.

For individuals who wish to live as fully as possible, it is important to realize that a static image of the body is not to be confused with the dynamic life of the body itself. The body reveals, to a considerable extent, the inner life of the person. The *image* of the body, in the form of an artificially cultivated pose, serves to conceal and restrict that life.

Once we become aware of the constricting and artificial quality of our cultivated poses, we may feel the need to free ourselves from an imaginary world which - like the world of the sorcerer's apprentice - has spun out of control. To do so, we must address the issue of changing our destructive habits.

Changing Habits

In his book, *Reconciliations,* Theodore Rubin writes that the endeavor to change habits which have existed over a long period of time is no simple task, and he points out that great struggle may be required to bring about such change. When we reflect on making changes, it is easy to minimize the challenges that such an undertaking may present. Part of the difficulty may result from the ambiguity in our use of the word "habit." We sometimes consider that a habit should be as easy to change as an article of clothing that can be discarded when it is worn out. In fact, the word "habit" can indeed be used to refer to clothing. As the dictionary suggests, a habit may be "the garb of a particular rank, profession, or religious order." Nonetheless, changing habits is not as easy as changing clothes. Habits represent longstanding dispositions and tendencies in personal behavior and experience. Such dispositions and tendencies often run deep.

51

Affirmation of Life

A habit may be more than a simple, isolated practice. Instances of specific, recurring behavior may, in fact, be an expression of an underlying imbalance in the structural and functional organization of the person. This would help to explain why habits are easier to change or abandon for one individual than for another. The crucial factor would be the degree of reinforcement of the particular habit in the underlying structure and experience of the person.

In his book, *The Potent Self*, Moshe Feldenkrais has defined character as "a preferred pattern of behavior, formed by each individual through personal experience of the environment." As Wilhelm Reich has so clearly shown, character and physical structure, considered dynamically, are functionally identical. Thus each of us, in the evolution of our personal history, develops a specific stance in life that is both uniquely our own and, at the same time, is related to the general social and cultural context that prevails. The history of our personal evolution is necessarily reflected in our posture. The degree of chronic spasticity or flaccidity in the various muscular segments of the body may be coupled with restricted patterns of respiration that are habitually present. Narrowly defined processes of association in the nervous system may go hand in hand with reduced flexibility of movement and constricted self-awareness. These are only some of the factors that combine to make up our personal structure. This structure provides the context in which undesired habits typically emerge and are sustained. Is it any wonder, then, that we sometimes feel that the habits we have may, in fact, "have us"?

It is not difficult to see why making changes in our lives can prove to be no simple and easy matter. Elsewhere I have addressed the issue of change in the following words: "Style, fashion, taste may change, but the individual himself does not. He merely doffs or dons a different garment, or spouse, or life-style, but nothing proceeds organically from within, originating in an impulse of creativity, changing the world." Such is bound to be the case when specific instances of undesired behavior and practice are viewed as subject to change without altering the underlying structure of which they are a part, and without effecting a re-education toward more meaningful and gratifying choices. Education in this sense means *educing* (bringing forth) a more relaxed, balanced, and dynamically energetic personal structure to serve as a more adequate basis for continued growth and development. This type of education is the opposite of that approach which has been aptly criticized by F.M. Alexander as "end-gaining."

There is an old saying that "experience is the best teacher." The tendency to repeat our mistakes in spite of ourselves is evidence of an habitual frame of reference with a limited range of choices. Such a situation reflects an inability to learn from experience. If this is true, however, in what manner can we reinvigorate our capacity to learn and grow? The answer suggested in the present argument is that patterns of chronic imbalance and distress in the habitual postural attitude of the person must be clarified and dissolved in order to bring about sufficient flexibility so that truly informed choices can be made. At the same time, improved functioning must be facilitated, especially at the deep level of more nearly optimal breathing, since improved respiration is related to increased personal energy, and adequate energy is necessary for a vigorous life. It is on the foundation of such a perspective that changes in specific habits may be seen to be related to changes in the overall pattern of structure and function that has evolved in the course of an individual's personal history.

Of the many benefits that may derive from confronting and changing self-destructive habits, perhaps none is more timely or more generally appreciated than the reduction of excessive stress in living.

The Treadmill of Stress

In his book, *The Healing Heart,* Norman Cousins presents an account of his recuperation from a severe heart attack. In that work, Cousins tells of his anxiety regarding a standard test of cardiac functioning involving the use of a treadmill to measure the response of the heart to a controlled expenditure of physical effort. In spite of the fact that such a test is an accepted medical means of evaluating the condition of the heart, Cousins felt that he could comfortably submit to the procedure only under circumstances that would allow him to reduce what we might call his "performance anxiety." His thinking concerning this subject was interesting. He reasoned that if he could operate the treadmill himself he would gain an increased sense of control and self-direction. Expressed in his own words, what Cousins had objected to in his previous use of the machine ".....was that the machine was running me; I wanted to run the machine."

In the world in which we live, it is common knowledge that most individuals are faced with an inordinate amount of stress in their lives. Over a period of several decades, there has been a steady increase in the attention paid to stress factors in the precipitation of major degenerative problems such as cardiovascular disease and cancer. Stress, however, is not itself pathological, though there is much evidence correlating excessive stress with medical problems. Stress is something which all of us face in our daily lives, and while it is the job of a medical doctor to diagnose and treat specific pathology, the task of avoiding the debilitating effects of excessive stress in our lives is the responsibility of each one of us. The following remarks are intended to focus on the nature of that task.

There are a number of different facets to the phenomenon of stress: cultural, social, psychological, emotional, and interpersonal, to name only a few. Stress, moreover, has a temporal dimension. We can become distressed with respect to anticipated future events, as well as with regard to present disturbances in our lives; and our present problems may be due, in part, to the continuation of self-destructive patterns of behavior acquired in the past. But just what is stress, this phenomenon which has become such a topic of interest?

This is not an easy question to answer, but for the purposes of our present discussion, we can say that stress is a condition resulting from a force or pressure which tends to cause a deformation or imbalance in the structure and function of the person. Since we are speaking here of a pressure or force which threatens the integrity of the individual, our use of the term "stress" is closely related to "distress." To return to the example of Norman Cousins, we could say that the mechanical treadmill which he used was intended to measure his heart's adaptation to stress. Cousins, however, found the experience of being on the treadmill distressful in itself, apart from the question of physical exertion. Is this not the case with most of us when it comes to dealing with the "treadmill" of contemporary social and personal pressures?

The solution which Norman Cousins devised to help diminish his distress in relation to the treadmill was to seek to control his exposure to that anxiety-producing procedure. Since the stressful and distressing nature of the world in which we live is not likely to be altered as rapidly as we might wish, there is wisdom in learning to gain as much reasonable and constructive control of our lives as possible. It is important to emphasize the words "reasonable" and "constructive" in this context, since a compulsive tendency toward excessive self-control is itself one of the distressing features of our contemporary way of being. If we genuinely wish to find ways to gain effective control of our lives, we may benefit by examining more closely the dynamics of stress as they are embodied concretely in the functioning of the individual. We can do this by considering the role of energy and balance. Taken together, these two factors provide a productive framework in terms of which the amelioration of stress can be viewed.

As human beings, all of us embody energy, and we require energy in order to live. The exact nature of biological energy is a controversial question, yet whatever our opinion regarding this matter, we can agree that the more energy we have available, functioning in a balanced and harmonious equilibrium, the stronger will be our ability to tolerate and contend with the stresses that impinge upon us. We can also understand that any forces which tend to deplete and exhaust our energy reserves will be harmful to our overall well-being and may serve to foster a vulnerability to stressor agents with which we come into contact. One common result of depleted energy is a more or less chronic state of fatigue. Another result of seriously diminished energy is a condition of habitual muscular tensions due to an over-concentration of effort to push and keep going in spite of the fact that such an effort does not come smoothly and naturally but requires will power.

Not only are stress and energy dynamics connected, but how we handle stress is related to the history of our personal development and the ways in which we have learned to deal with situations in which there is a strong element of conflict. It is not without significance that in human beings stress beyond the natural level tolerated - and, indeed, needed - by our organisms is experienced as conflict. The history of our conflicts is embodied in the patterns of chronic muscular tension, or armor, that delineate our basic posture in life. The patterns of forced and restricted respiration that correspond to these tensions and imbalances must be dissolved in order to liberate a new tolerance for greater energy and more potent living. If this can be achieved, then one may hope for more than just "coping" or "adjustment" in response to the stresses of modern life. The real goal becomes to increase our capacity to learn, grow, and live in a meaningful and fulfilling manner.

In these times when "stress" has become a household word and "stress management" is promoted and sought by many, we should not forget that life is more than just the absence of stress. No one need conclude that this means that we should simply ignore the hazards of excessive stress. Nor should we fail to value the ability to cope with the inevitable difficulties of life. But the mere reduction of stress is not itself ultimately fulfilling. After all, a dead person presumably feels no stress at all, but death is not a condition actively desired by most of us. In fact, as Norman Cousins has observed in his book, death is tragic only when our life has lost its meaning. Cousins remarks: "Death is not the enemy; living in constant fear of it is."

One of the more creative responses on the part of humans to the excessive stresses of life in the world today entails an ongoing struggle and commitment to expand, deepen, and enhance more natural energetic functioning. This may require working through significant conflicts which embody our personal history, deform our personal structure, and restrict our personal growth. While such an undertaking is not easy, it is meaningful. A consideration of the rationale and feasibility of such a venture raises issues which go to the "heart of the matter."

The Heart of the Matter

In one of his works, Henry Miller writes of his desire to alleviate the inordinate suffering of human beings; but in order to do so, he reflects, he would have to be able to change the hearts of men, a seemingly impossible task. Since the days when Miller wrote, we have come to live in an age in which technological sophistication has made startling and complex feats possible, including the implantation of artificial hearts into human beings. Yet the meaning and significance of the dilemma expressed by Henry Miller - and by Dostoevski before him - have not diminished. In an important sense, being able to open our hearts to the feeling of life is an answer to suffering, since to maintain an open heart involves an acceptance of the human condition. In the world in which we live, this may be no easy task, even if an open heart is seen to be the domain of wisdom. But what does it mean to speak of the "wisdom of the heart"?

Certainly, one way to view the heart is as a pump, and most people are aware that, physiologically, this is the heart's prime function. By pumping blood to the tissues, the heart supplies the body with oxygen, and it eliminates waste products by pumping deoxygenated blood to the lungs, where carbon dioxide is expelled in exhalation. Alexander Lowen, however, has commented on the limited range of such an understanding of the heart. In his book, *Bioenergetics,* he states: "The richness of expression involving the word heart shows how important its extramechanical aspects are to people." Lowen points out that such terms as the "heart of life" and the "heart of the matter" are common expressions that may be taken seriously to refer to the depth of human self-awareness that has its center of feeling in the region of the actual physical organ of the heart. Lowen argues, in fact, that the heart may be considered to be the core of the person. It is difficult to conceive of the heart as being one of the important centers of feeling in the body if one takes a strictly mechanical view of reality. To adopt such an exclusively mechanical view, however, involves dissociating oneself from ones bodily feelings. This type of dissociation, as Wilhelm Reich has made clear, is unfortunately one of the defining characteristics of our epoch.

To suggest that the heart lies at the core of our being does not mean that we can realistically dispense with all modes of awareness that do not arise directly from that center. We may desire a heart-felt appreciation for life and a hearty existence, but we will suffer only a "bleeding heart" if the reality of the rest of our functioning as human beings is not respected. Lowen's way of acknowledging the relationship of the heart to the whole self is to state that "every heart needs a head which will provide it with eyes and ears so it can be in touch with reality." In the same vein, we need also to have our feet on the ground so that we can take a stand; and if we endeavor to follow a "path with heart," as some have recommended, then we will have to have a substantial capacity for healthy struggle, intelligence, commitment, and aggression in order to avoid needless pain and suffering. The heart thus finds its true context within the totality of the living person, not in disembodied sacrifice.

The heart of experience involves contact at a bodily level with sensations that are centered in the region of the thorax. These sensations are real, not imagined, and their perception entails a certain degree of mobility of the chest as it participates in the pulsatory process of respiration. We may be more or less closed to the demands and needs of the heart. Or we may experience the particular joy that comes with an increased feeling of openness in that segment of the body. In all events, the process of growth and change, challenging as it is, surely is a matter of the heart, just as surely as the heart finds its true home in the relatively integrated functioning of the person as a whole. Concern for the wisdom of the heart, therefore, is a natural human condition.

In his book, *The Facts of Life,* R. D. Laing comments: "A mechanical man has a pump, a heartless pump. If the heart is a pump, show me a pump with a heart." If we are aware of the importance of heart-felt experience in human life, then we may well ask why such experience is so evidently difficult to cultivate and sustain. Part of the reason may be, paradoxically, our fear of experiencing and expressing the so-called "negative" emotions in life.

The Negative and the Positive

It is generally the case that individuals are capable of identifying elements in their personal experience which they look upon either with favor or disapproval. Interestingly, however, there is a great degree of variability in the characteristics that people accept or reject in themselves. One individual may, for example, feel that anger - virtually any expression of anger - is abhorrent. Such an individual will be likely to view humility, compassion, and tolerance as the cardinal virtues. There are other persons, nonetheless, who have little apparent difficulty in venting anger and in taking an assertive stance in life. Such individuals may well consider sympathy, openness, and concern to be evidence of weakness. As the old saying suggests: "One man's meat is another man's poison." Yet this does not help to clarify the considerable disparity among differing people's attitudes toward some of the fundamental elements of human experience. How these differing attitudes arise is an interesting subject that reaches to the roots of human growth and development. Such growth and development, in turn, are intimately associated with pleasure and pain.

It is possible to argue that pleasure and pain are not operative at the deepest levels of nature. In the last century, Friedrich Nietzsche advanced the view that pleasure and pain are mere "epiphenomena" arising out of more primitive levels of biological organization. Yet if we consider pleasure and pain in relation to the overall functioning of the person, it is surely true that, for human beings, those aspects of experience which we consider positive are those that provide us with the greatest degree of genuine pleasure. The elements of experience which, in turn, we consider negative are those which involve pain and anxiety. Wilhelm Reich, on the basis of this understanding, was able to equate biological pleasure with movements of living organisms *"toward* the world." He classified anxiety, on the other hand, as functionally identical with movements *"away* from the world." In simple language, human beings reach out to genuine pleasure and shrink away from the prospect of pain. Humans share this type of behavior with simpler life forms, such as the amoeba, which extends its pseudopodia toward a positive stimulus (such as food) and withdraws its pseudopodia in response to a negative stimulus (such as contact with a sharp object). In the background of all human evaluations of "positive" and "negative" is to be found the fundamental antithesis between the deep biological experiences of pleasure and anxiety. It is this antithesis which underlies the cultural and personal conditioning on the basis of which each individual elaborates his or her unique personal history.

In his book, *The Elusive Obvious,* Moshe Feldenkrais takes a position very similar to that of Wilhelm Reich. The specific vantage point adopted by Feldenkrais is a consideration of the human nervous system. He suggests that the contact of the newborn infant with the outside world is mediated primarily through that part of the brain known as the sensory cortex. In the beginning, the reality of the baby is essentially a sensory, subjective one. We would say that the infant is identified with sensory stimuli emanating from deep within its own organism. Feldenkrais points out that gradually, in a step-by-step fashion, the subjective reality of the child will "....give way to a slowly growing complex of sensations of a special kind - sensations which surrounding people approve or condemn." Even the most basic bodily activities and functions will be shaped and molded under the pressure of critical evaluations on the part of adults. Feldenkrais remarks: "By and by, it will dawn on the new apprentice to adulthood that some of his most cherished subjective reality is not acceptable to those who provide his needs and above all the security of forthcoming care and affection." It is in the midst of such circumstances that most individuals learn to accept and reject significant aspects of their own personal experience. As Feldenkrais illustrates, the results of this learning process become anchored in the neurological functioning of the person and involve the formation of a specific self-image accompanied by restricted patterns of movement and a limited degree of self-awareness.

For those who are disturbed by personal limitations resulting from a difficult individual history, the question arises: how is it possible to untie the "Gordian knot" of our habitual patterns of restricted movement, sensation, awareness, and thinking? How can we achieve a greater depth and range of experience? The fact that human beings are not born with a rigidly fixed set of behavioral responses to the environment serves as the basis for attempting to further the growth and learning process in a positive direction, even if considerable adversity has been the rule during the formative, early years of life. Such a direction necessarily involves changes in posture, movement, organismic motility, sensation, awareness, and self-image, all of which must be rooted in a deepened understanding of oneself. To accomplish such a reorientation involves confronting an ironic truth: often as not, our "virtues" are the seat of our problems. Our "vices," on the other hand, are frequently the source of our untapped potential. Thus, in order to achieve a more balanced perspective, the "humble" person will need to reclaim his or her abandoned aggression. In contrast, the compulsively aggressive person will need to discover the capacity to surrender. In both instances, we may suspect that anxiety will be associated with such changes in behavior, for anxiety was at the root of our initial denial of important aspects of our own functioning. Our original anxiety must, therefore, be resurrected, confronted, and worked through in the process of uncovering our buried potential.

The desire to disentangle ourselves from the constraints that bind our capacity for increased pleasure and meaning in life is not a product of wishful thinking. It is eminently reasonable to attempt to discover and potentiate the organic sources of pleasure and energetic self-expression that go hand in hand with an acceptance of our biological core. An undertaking of this type is an adventure which involves confronting and assimilating those genuine aspects of our personal experience which have been excluded from acceptability. In this manner, a truly potent personal identification with life can unfold, allowing for the rationality of both the positive and the negative in our experience, depending on the nature of the circumstances in which we find ourselves.

The potential rewards of such an undertaking justify the inevitable anxiety that emerges at certain stages along the way. Such anxiety presents a challenge.

The Challenge of Anxiety

Anyone who seriously attempts to understand the human condition must take into account the phenomenon of anxiety. Perhaps no state of experience is so universally avoided as this one. Yet anxiety - along with its counterpart, pleasure - is at the basis of all human behavior. Much of our contemporary cultural orientation can be understood as an attempt to deaden anxiety. Certainly, an excessive use of harmful drugs and intoxicants is an instance of avoidance behavior. Indeed, the truth would appear to be that almost any activity can be used in order to avoid anxiety. Thus the fervent mystic may retreat into an inner world of images and symbols in an attempt to escape the stress of dealing with the pressures of present-day social existence. The compulsive materialist, on the other hand, may engage in an all-consuming pursuit of success in business or science as a means of canceling out an inner feeling of emptiness and futility. The multiplicity of methods which human beings employ to deaden anxiety is reflected in the variability of human character structure. Nonetheless, underlying the many ways in which individuals attempt to cope with their uneasiness is the single phenomenon: anxiety. How are we to define this condition, and what are we to make of it?

If we take as our starting point the etymology of the word, anxiety simply refers to a "troubled state of mind." The quality of feeling which is involved in anxiety is often one of intense fear and dread. The philosopher, Søren Kierkegaard, aptly characterized this emotional state in the titles of two of his books - *Fear and Trembling* and *The Sickness unto Death.* Indeed, anxiety may entail great apprehension and anguish. The word "anguish" is derived from the Latin *angustiae,* meaning a "tight place." When we are anxious we are "up tight." At the same time, we may experience trembling, sweating, and an extreme degree of agitation. In German, the word for anxiety is *Angst,* which means a "choking in the narrows." A sense of anxiety is conveyed by images of being "hemmed in," "confined in a tight place," "choked," or "trapped." Such images, I would suggest, refer to the actual functional state of the organism which is "gripped" by the experience of anxiety. The actuality of these expressions can be appreciated if we examine the function of anxiety in nature.

While anxiety is sometimes considered to be a uniquely human trait, the roots of this emotional response can be seen in extremely simple organisms. The ordinary garden slug, for example, extends its antennae in a groping, sensing manner as it moves its head in an exploratory fashion. If I move my index finger close to one of the antennae, it is not necessary for me even to touch the little animal in order to elicit a response. The presence of my finger is detected by the slug, and the antennae quickly retract. After a moment or two, if I remove my finger, the antennae will protrude again. Similar responses are true of the sea anemone, which can be observed at the beach. Descriptions of like behavior on the part of the amoeba can be found in zoology texts. We may say that the slug, the sea anemone, and the amoeba all exhibit what amounts to an anxiety reaction when provoked by a negative stimulus. The essence of that reaction is to contract, to draw into oneself, to shrink, to become narrower. Since none of the organisms described here has any chance to fight back or to run away, contraction is, under the circumstances, an optimal response to danger.

In spite of their relative biological complexity, human beings display the same basic responses to threatening situations that are found in less developed organisms. In dangerous circumstances, our possible behavior is limited essentially to three alternatives: fight, flight, or compromise. In nature, the agitated and troubled state of awareness that is indicative of anxiety prepares the organism for activity. In humans, the adrenal glands are activated, and the sympathetic branch of the autonomic nervous system becomes dominant, readying the body for exertion. Blood is rushed to the skeletal muscles, which contract somewhat in the manner of springs in anticipation of the thrust that will take place in attack or retreat. The responses of the human being at this level are involuntary. This is necessary, since in a true natural emergency we do not have time to think and deliberate. The tendency during an emergency is for more recently evolved structures within the nervous system to yield to more primitive areas which are situated in what is known as the "old brain."

The real problem facing human beings is not the presence of anxiety as a natural, organismic response to danger; rather, it is the prevalence of environmental conditions in which the natural response of anxiety no longer serves its original function of protection. It is now known that prolonged exposure to distressful situations will induce in living organisms a pattern of reaction that has been characterized by the endocrinologist, Hans Selye, as the General Adaptation Syndrome. This patterned response to prolonged situations of distress involves an initial alarm reaction, followed by a period of resistance, culminating in exhaustion and death. It is interesting to speculate to what extent the General Adaptation Syndrome may be functionally identical with anxiety on a basic biological level, but that issue need not be decided in the present context. It is enough to recognize that a state of chronic anxiety acts as a stressor which necessarily provokes the General Adaptation Syndrome, with potentially dire consequences for the well-being of human organisms. Unfortunately, as many investigators have pointed out, the present social and cultural context in which most human beings find themselves is one in which there are significant factors exposing individuals to a more or less constant sense of danger. Since these factors are structurally embedded in the general cultural setting, they present challenges and problems that are not subject to immediate resolution by means of the spontaneous enactment of the fight-or-flight response. Human beings are thus faced with a dilemma. The environment in which they find themselves is at odds with their own deep-seated biological reflexes. What does such a situation portend?

Leaving aside the interesting and important question of how such a social and cultural situation has come about, it seems clear that the problem of chronic anxiety in contemporary life is related to the inadequate conditions for growth and development which are encountered by most individuals in childhood. One of the significant facts concerning the withdrawal response of living organisms subjected to negative stimuli is that the withdrawn condition tends to become structured into the organism if it is elicited repeatedly. Thus the amoeba, the sea anemone, and the slug are inclined to maintain themselves in a state of contraction if their functioning is threatened time after time. The same phenomenon holds true in the case of human beings. The growing child who is threatened repeatedly with anxiety-producing situations will assume a posture which is habitually contracted. Such a posture, which serves as a kind of armor, acts to protect the organism by deadening the experience of distress.

Given the fact that our contemporary culture is fraught with dangers that seem to be ongoing and relentless, it is understandable that there is a strong disposition in many people to deny the experience of anxiety and to avoid the challenge which this basic emotion represents. Under the circumstances, however, it is in our interest to learn to recognize our anxiety and to identify those aspects of modern life which produce in us a sense of dread. This is true even if many of the distressing features of our contemporary existence seem to be beyond our immediate and direct control. By staying in touch with our anxiety, we can attempt to do what is in our power to prevent ourselves from becoming emotionally exhausted. We also can seek to take action within the domain of our immediate surroundings to make life more meaningful, and we can work to provide our children with a healthier upbringing than the one which we ourselves may have experienced. In the pursuit of these goals, it may be helpful, or even necessary, to find a constructive context in which we can work through our inner personal conflicts which have accumulated as a result of the anxieties that were part of our individual developmental history. In any event, the success of our struggle to understand the human condition and to improve the circumstances of our lives depends on our capacity to face the challenge of anxiety.

The failure to face the challenge of anxiety draws many problems in its wake. On a personal level, one such problem that has been identified is the phenomenon popularly referred to as "burnout."

Burnout and Personal Growth

Only that which is on fire can be said to "burn out." In this sense, the term "burnout" has been used by several authors to refer to a state of exhaustion, disillusionment, and malaise that occurs after an initial period of excitement, commitment, and enthusiasm. Used in this way, the term "burnout" refers not simply to a state of exhaustion that results from defending oneself against too great a stress for too long a time. Rather, burnout involves the disappointment of certain positive expectations that have been aggressively set for oneself. While the person who "burns out" may be exhausted, the condition itself results from the failure to achieve goals. This is why, according to various studies, the so-called "underachiever" does not burn out. Burnout does not occur without a degree of passion and commitment. If burnout is a common feature of contemporary life, as evidence suggests is the case, then what can be done to safeguard the fires of life so that the flame remains bright? We may even ask the following question: is it not possible that an awareness of becoming "burned out" can lead to a positive renewal of energetic functioning and personal growth?

In all human situations, understanding is an essential tool in learning to weigh the costs and rewards of our behavior. In the case of burnout, it is important to recognize the signs of the condition. Chronic fatigue and frustration, accumulated over a period of time in response to failed expectations, are one important sign. In his book, *Burnout: The High Cost of Achievement*, Herbert Freudenberger has written that whenever the level of an individual's expectations comes into conflict with the limitations of reality, and the individual does not modify his expectations, "trouble is on the way." Freudenberger comments that in such a situation, deep within the person, "attrition is building up, the inevitable result of which will be the depletion of the individual's resources, an attrition of his vitality, energy, and ability to function." Understanding that burnout is a common phenomenon in today's world is one way to help to avoid the debilitating experience of becoming exhausted and dispirited. It is easier to avoid a danger to our well-being if we are aware of the threat in the first place. Some relief can be had by acknowledging what a common problem burnout is.

Once the signs of burnout are identified, various steps may be taken to alter the balance of stressful forces that are contributing to a person's sense of malaise. There are, however, really only three alternatives. One possibility is that individual expectations, attitudes, and habits may be altered in order to relieve some of the disappointment concerning the failure of anticipated developments to materialize. This may be understood as becoming more realistic with respect to the possibility of accomplishing specific goals. Another possibility is to alter the context in which we attempt to achieve our aims. In this way, the objective situation may be changed in order to make our expectations more realistic. What is impossible in one set of circumstances may be feasible under other conditions. The third alternative involves a combination of personal change and environmental change. This option is likely to be called for when the area of disappointment in our lives reaches down into the fundamental issues that define our personal identity.

Once the nature of burnout has been clarified, an interesting observation can be made. Such an observation is stated by Ayala Pines and Elliot Aronson in their book, *Burnout: From Tedium to Personal Growth*. The authors note that individuals vary greatly in their fundamental attitudes toward life, in their personal needs and priorities, and in their ability to handle stress. They then point out that "these and other intervening variables can influence when burnout will occur, how long it will last, and how severe its consequences will be." If we wish to extend the line of reasoning of these authors, we must ask: what factors in an individual's make-up incline him or her in the direction of chronic burnout? An answer to that question is suggested by a consideration of individual growth and development and the manner in which that growth and development are embodied in the structural and functional balance and posture of the person.

Seen from a functional, dynamic standpoint, the resiliency of an individual's energies, the capacity to clarify a stressful situation, and the impulse toward a meaningful and realistic engagement in life's tasks are all related to the developmental history as well as the present-day attitude of the person. A human being's specific history and contemporary attitude, however, are not merely incidental to his or her make-up. On the contrary, they are anchored and expressed in the vital functioning of the person. Practically, this means that how much energy we have available to accomplish a given objective and how we go about our task are intimately related to the quality of our habitual respiratory patterns and the degree of chronic muscular tension affecting the range of our movements and the depth of our self-awareness. It is common knowledge that what is "realistic" for one individual may be "illusory" for another. In any case, the capacity to breathe and feel deeply and to employ a wide range of movements and options in our personal activity is the most satisfactory basis for evaluating the wisdom of a given endeavor. We may choose to fight. We may choose to run. We may choose to compromise. We may combine all three of these options in a complex situation. It is unlikely that we will allow ourselves to "burn out" if we preserve contact with our vital functioning.

If we were to ask what is the most common type of burnout situation, the answer might be that there is a prevailing contemporary tendency to burn out on "life." People in certain roles - such as nurses, and people in the helping professions in general - have been shown to suffer a higher than average incidence of burnout. At some level, however, all of us have expectations of life. For too many of us, these expectations come to be viewed as incapable of realization. The problem may be due in significant measure to the unrealistic nature of our expectations. If our desire, however, is to live deeply and fully, we may need to establish the capacity for more satisfactory personal functioning in such a manner as to deepen and expand our breathing, increase our energy, and establish a more balanced and less stressful organization of our personal structure. To do this is synonymous with increasing our capacity to recognize and put into effect life-affirmative choices. If this is the case, then the experience of burnout, or the awareness of the danger of burning out, may serve as the impetus not just for a minor personal adjustment, but for serious transformation in our lives. It is likely that such transformation will involve an increased appreciation for the place of creativity in personal growth.

Creativity and Personal Growth

In the corner of one of his paintings, the artist Paul Gauguin has inscribed three questions: Where do we come from? What are we? Where are we going? These are the perennial issues which human beings must face, and it may be that the significance of life for human beings lies not so much in answering these questions as in posing them. Taken together, these questions suggest something of the mystery of life. The human animal, of all creatures, reflects upon his condition. Children, as they become increasingly aware of themselves and the world around them, spontaneously wonder about the same issues that Gauguin pondered. As human beings, we seek answers to the problems of existence, and we look for our individual place in the scheme of things. In doing so, we often arrive at definite conclusions regarding the nature of life. The roots of our understanding of the universal questions of life asked by Gauguin and others are to be found in the soil of our personal existence. How we ask the important questions of life - whether in fear or anger, gratitude or excitement - is an indication of the course we will take in our future development. At the same time, our manner of asking these questions reflects our experience on the road we have already traveled. What key factors, then, are crucial in determining our view of life?

As many people are aware, Paul Gauguin became disenchanted with the world of Western civilization as it was developing in the modern era. His disillusionment was shared by other now well-known figures of the same period. Seeking escape from Europe, Gauguin sailed to Tahiti, where he hoped to discover primitive people in touch with a more natural way of living. Many of his paintings reflect his vision of such a way of life. In a similar fashion, the writer D.H. Lawrence embarked upon what has been called his "savage pilgrimage" in which he traveled around the world in search of a more harmonious type of existence. Both Gauguin and Lawrence were ultimately disappointed in their quest. Two reasons for their disillusionment readily come to mind. On the one hand, Gauguin and Lawrence were products of the culture which they sought to flee, and they therefore carried within themselves the contradictions inherent in that culture. On the other hand, Lawrence and Gauguin, as well as others like them, found that they had been preceded in their journey by colonizers representing the official Western cultural and social milieu - the very order these artists were attempting to escape. The world of Gauguin and Lawrence's imagination was not to be found by them in reality.

Today, it is generally acknowledged that a more primitive and less anxiety-ridden way of life - however one may picture such a state - is no simple matter to find. Yet the questions posed by Gauguin retain their original force: Where do we come from? What are we? Where are we going? Many persons have grappled with these questions. One such individual was Wilhelm Reich, the former associate of Sigmund Freud, who set out on his own to investigate the nature of living functioning.

In the course of his work with clients, and as a result of his observation of the social scene of his day, Reich came to the conclusion that the problems of contemporary living are inescapable as long as each new generation of human beings is shaped and molded according to the values and priorities of a destructive social and cultural order. Exactly how such a shaping and molding process occurs was understood by Reich in an original way. In Reich's view, debilitating social and cultural pressures are anchored in patterns of disrupted personal functioning which are learned primarily during the early, formative period of an individual's life. Such patterns of disturbed functioning can be seen to affect basic biological processes, such as respiration, posture, movement, feeling, and emotional expressiveness. Once learned, these patterns - even though they are destructive of personal well-being - are experienced as "second nature." This explains, in part, why such patterns of disrupted functioning are in practice difficult to change. The individual resists letting go of these patterns, because letting go is perceived as a threat to the person's identity. The problem of the alienation of culture was thus seen by Reich to be, at the same time, a problem of disturbed individual functioning. In this light, the struggle of the individual against the stressful and destructive aspects of contemporary culture also involves the struggle to become free of the stressful and destructive aspects of ones own personal functioning. One goal of such a struggle is to allow the natural impulses of life within oneself to emerge. On the basis of the experience of these impulses, one can take a more genuinely positive view of existence under the difficult circumstances which are the common fate of contemporary human beings. It is precisely the expression of such uninhibited, natural impulses which attracts us to the more compelling works of artists such as Gauguin and Lawrence. The power of their own living impulses is the basis for these artists' creativity. What does it mean, however, to be creative?

No one can give a conclusive answer to that question. It seems reasonable, however, to argue that the more in touch a person is with the true feelings and drives which are the source of living experience, the more will creative potential be available to the individual. Part of such creativity involves struggling in the course of daily living to actualize as nearly as possible ones deepest and most natural motivations. In this sense, each person - whether or not that person is an artist - must seek to come to grips with Gauguin's questions. This is a challenging task, yet for human beings the alternative is nihilism - a loss of faith in the value of life itself.

A valid response to the challenges of life must be worked out by each individual, and it would not be appropriate for a functional, energetic discipline, which stresses the worth of personal creativity, to be overly directive with respect to specific modes of behavior. What can be said, however, is that any genuine movement in the direction of more integrated functioning will tend to bring about a greater self-reliance on the part of the individual when it comes to facing the fundamental issues of living. In this regard, achieving abstract answers is not the main concern. Rather, it is how we respond concretely to life's problems that matters. Another way of saying the same thing is to state that our answers to life's basic questions are embodied in how we live. This refers literally to the quality of our bodily motility, to our breathing, movement, posture, and self-expression. It is on the basis of such fundamental aspects of human functioning that our creative impulses strive to respond to the difficult yet essential questions of life.

Returning to the three questions posed by Gauguin in his painting, it is evident that the criticisms which that artist leveled at the civilization of his day were directed at some basic aspects of the social world which remain in force in the present. To look more deeply into these aspects of social life leads to a consideration of such matters as power, potency, and pleasure.

Power, Potency, and Pleasure

In the life of the individual, there is a relationship between power, potency, and pleasure. The precise nature of this relationship, however, is not as simple as might at first appear to be the case. In terms of popular culture, potency is measured on the basis of success, and pleasure is seen to be the result of power. Thus the individual who has large sums of money can buy power, achieve success, and obtain pleasure; and this, in turn, is thought to serve as proof of potency. Similarly, the powerful person will commonly attempt to amass a fortune in order to purchase pleasure and acquire status. Again, the result is thought to be potency. While it is clear that not all individuals see reality in these terms, it is only fair to acknowledge that in our contemporary society great pressure is exerted on people to adopt such an outlook. Almost all mass advertising makes use of images of power, potency, and pleasure in order to sell commodities. This is true whether the product being sold is a basic item of utility such as a piece of furniture or a toothbrush, or a luxury article such as an expensive automobile or an exotic vacation. As one billboard message proclaims: "Success is the best revenge!" Advertising of this kind would not be successful as a motivating factor, however, if some element were not present tempting many people to subscribe to such a view. I would suggest that the element in question is a widespread sense of powerlessness and a lack of genuine pleasure in contemporary living. At the core of such a situation is the experience of personal impotence.

The terms "power" and "potency" are etymologically related. At the root of both words is the Latin verb, *posse,* meaning "to be able." The words "possibility" and "potential" are derived from the same source. We might say that power, potency, possibility, and potential are all expressions of the same condition. Yet how are we to understand that condition? Is it not the case that the state of being which underlies the authentic experience to which these words refer is the condition of being "able to live?"

According to my experience and observation, the overall emphasis on power which is prevalent in today's culture reflects, in part, the need to compensate for a lack of potency. Thus an individual may seek to acquire wealth in the expectation that this will bring pleasure. While few would deny that a basic amount of material goods is necessary for the satisfaction of fundamental human needs, material goods and status can provide only a *symbol* of personal success. There is a limit to how many goods any individual can consume, and a symbol cannot adequately substitute for reality. This is why so many individuals become disappointed after they achieve their goals. Their achievement cannot compensate for a lack of gratification of genuine, human needs. Often, in the struggle for success, authentic possibilities for fulfillment are shoved aside. In place of fulfillment, there is a preoccupation with power, which is understood as "being in control." Such power, at the social level, may bring public status at the price of personal meaning.

If the present analysis is accurate, we must then ask why individuals would choose to sacrifice genuine potency for power, status, and control. The answer lies, no doubt, in the personal history of the individual who makes such a sacrifice. No individual who experiences the pleasure of truly satisfying functioning will lightly bargain away that pleasure for an image of success. Many people, however, desire to be "somebody" because at heart they feel that they are "nobody." The evidence suggests that such a feeling is based on a person's experience of having been rejected in terms of his or her basic bodily functions, which are the source of real pleasure in life. Among these functions are good breathing, an adequate level of personal energy, a relatively balanced and graceful coordination of movement patterns, and the ability to form personal relationships founded on genuine contact and emotional openness. Where the validity of these functions has been rejected, substitute satisfactions must be sought. Yet there is no adequate substitute for life, and such a venture is foredoomed. Since a reasonable adult is unlikely to relinquish genuine pleasure and human potency in exchange for a paltry substitute, what accounts for such current personal and cultural trends? The answer must be sought in the childhood situation.

No child is in a position to choose freely his or her attitude toward life. As children, we are all dependent upon adults for nurturing. This dependence is primarily in relation to our parents or to parent substitutes. If our basic needs for acceptance, respect, love, support, and guidance are met, we will learn to identify with our natural functioning at a bodily level, and we will grow up to become independent persons. In this case, we will literally understand ourselves to be "some-body." On the other hand, if our functioning is unnecessarily interfered with, we will lose some of our capacity to stand up to the demands of life. Unable to rely on our bodily experience, we will feel ourselves to be "at a loss," and we will seek to make up for that loss through compensatory activities - such as the struggle for power, success, or revenge. Pleasure and potency, however, are natural conditions of undisturbed functioning and cannot be acquired except by means of identifying with our basic bodily processes.

It is not necessary to become a "success" in order to experience the disillusionment that stems from the idolization of power. The individual who fails after a lifetime of struggle may be just as committed to substitute satisfactions as the person who "makes it." The problem is not with success, nor is it with struggle. Genuine struggle is part of life, and if we wish to live, we will seek to struggle successfully on life's terms. On the other hand, there must necessarily be a sense of failure which accompanies the struggle for compensatory rewards meant to supply meaning for an empty existence. That sense of failure is related to the fact that in such an undertaking we are struggling against our own true needs. Ironically, the person who has been more or less successful in this dubious task sometimes faces the greatest challenge. It requires courage, in such an instance, to face ones failure and gain an understanding of ones authentic needs and possibilities. It is only on the basis of the potency of a pleasurable and meaningful life, however, that power can come to mean being able to live in terms of our true potential. If we gain this ability, we are then enabled to see more clearly and to guard against the splits and conflicts which abound in our contemporary milieu. One such split is the dichotomy between the experiential alternatives of being "hard" and being "soft."

Being Hard and Being Soft

In the modern world, being "soft" and being "hard" represent two possible approaches to life. It is curious that both of these terms often are perceived to have negative connotations. The soft person is considered to be weak, and the hard person is thought to be unfeeling. On the other hand, we also recognize that being soft and being hard can be appropriate forms of behavior. Thus, we respect the person who can take a "hard look" at reality, and we appreciate the person who has a "soft spot" for the gentler aspects of life. It seems fairly obvious, upon reflection, that the capacity to be both soft and hard is a valuable human quality. Why, then, is there so much confusion and partisanship concerning the respective values of these two ways of being? Perhaps the answer lies in the fact that in so many cases human beings do not have the ability to be both hard and soft, as the circumstances demand. In such instances, the chronically hard or soft attitude of a person can best be understood as a defensive posture.

As most people are aware, human beings have a tendency to make a virtue out of necessity. As Nietzsche commented, memory and pride are often at odds, and pride usually wins. Most of us find certain aspects of our own personal history painful to face. Thus the person who is afraid to be aggressive will often pride himself on being "objective" and considerate of the other person's point of view. In this manner, fear is converted into broad-mindedness, and an unpleasant truth about oneself is replaced with a flattering falsehood. By the same token, the person who cannot surrender to his feelings will view his own rigidity and stiffness as strengths. In this way, fear of feeling is rationalized as a strong will. What, however, is the value of being considerate toward others if one is inconsiderate toward oneself? And what good is a strong will if one has no feeling for life? Ironically, both the chronically "hard" and the habitually "soft" individual share an underlying fear of self-expression and a refusal to tolerate genuine emotion.

A further irony which characterizes the plight of the person who is habitually hard or soft is the tendency toward self-rejection. This tendency, however, is denied, and instead of accepting the existence of self-hatred, the person finds fault with others who manifest some unwanted quality or trait. On one occasion, for example, I spoke with a woman who prided herself on being strong. She also set great store by her narrow waist, which she maintained by a regimen of daily sit-ups. Her problem, however, was an inability to soften up, and her romantic relationships consequently suffered. Nevertheless, she spoke disdainfully of women who allow their abdomens to become soft. It was clear that the disdain she expressed was secretly directed at her own inner softness, which she could not allow to be revealed. If she relaxed her abdomen, she was afraid of being hurt.

The qualities of being "hard" and being "soft" are literally expressed in the body structure of the person. At one extreme, the posture of the person who is excessively soft has virtually collapsed. There is insufficient resiliency or tonus in the soft tissues of the body to give the person flexibility and strength. At the opposite end of the spectrum, the rigid, impervious person reveals a musculature which may sometimes seem almost like granite to the touch. The large, skeletal muscles of such a person are in a state of chronic contraction. Needless to say, the breathing dictated by such a structure is controlled and shallow, and there is a tendency to hold the breath in the inspiratory position. The individual whose structure is soft will absorb a great deal of insult without responding aggressively. The rigid person, in contrast, will often act aggressively without provocation in order to ward off an imagined threat. The virtue of the excessively soft person is claimed to be sensitivity. In reality, this sensitivity tends to amount to sentimentality. The hard person normally advertises his virtues as strength and courage. In actuality, such strength and courage may be little more than stubbornness and lack of feeling.

If we look beyond the superficiality of the chronically soft or chronically hard way of being, I suspect that most of us would agree that an integrated balance is what we would like to attain. In today's world, such a goal is not easy to achieve, for the person who exhibits softness is often viewed as a sucker, and the individual who takes a hard look at life may be accused of cynicism. In order to reach a state of balance, rigid attitudes must be softened, and the ability to act aggressively with feeling must be strengthened. In this regard, one is reminded of the words of the poet, Arthur Rimbaud: "Because they were strong, they were gentle."

There can be little doubt that the excessively soft and the exaggeratedly hard person have much in common, though neither would readily admit it. The underlying reality for both types of individuals is anxiety (Fig. 7). If we are to move in the direction of enhanced integration, in spite of our fear, it is necessary to comprehend that often that which we most abhor represents an aspect of our own hidden potential. A tender heart and the capacity for aggression need not be mutually exclusive (Fig. 8). The mistake which is so frequently made is to view life in terms of mutually exclusive extremes. True, the person who is incapable of aggression must experience fury in order to regain strength, and the rigid person must become able to surrender in order to attain flexibility. These experiences, however, are part of a process of growth and integration that leads to balance. Naturally, that process of integration occurs most satisfactorily as part of the normal growth experience of the healthy child. When such an experience has not been forthcoming, it becomes our task to find alternative means to stimulate and support the renewal of the interrupted developmental process. In this fashion, we may seek to recover our true strength and sensitivity. In doing so, we will inevitably face the challenge of confronting our own resistance to change.

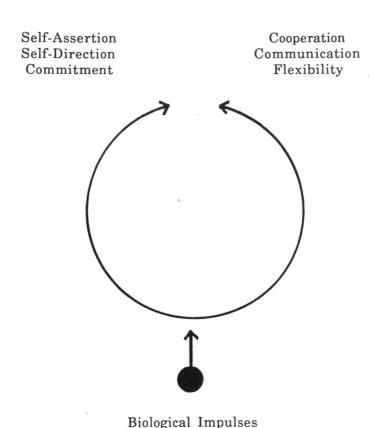

Self-Assertion
Self-Direction
Commitment

Cooperation
Communication
Flexibility

Biological Impulses

Figure #7: Emotional Responses Integrated

When natural biological impulses are free-flowing, the individual is capable of genuine self-assertion as well as cooperative endeavor. Strength and gentleness are complementary. Aggression is available for rational goals.

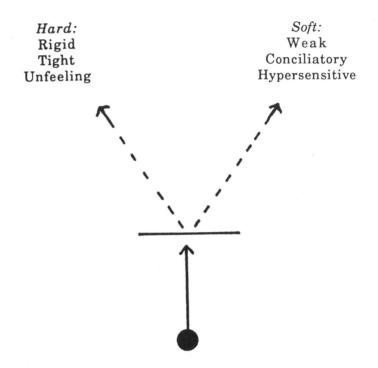

Biological Impulses

Figure #8: Emotional Responses Split

When basic biological impulses are blocked due to armoring, the unity of the organism is split into conflicting tendencies. The prevailing tendency will be reflected in a condition of either excessive "hardness" or compulsive "softness."

Confronting Resistances

As human beings, we are all faced with the necessity of learning and growing. The reason that growth and learning are a necessity for human beings, and not a luxury, is that the instincts of *Homo sapiens* are few in comparison to the instinctual endowments of other animals. This paucity of inborn, unconditioned responses creates both advantages and problems for our species. What is beyond question is that the comparative lack of instinctually determined behavior patterns in humans is correlated with a significant increase in the role of learning in the life of each person. In order to survive, individuals must adjust themselves to the demands of their environment. Especially during the formative years of childhood, such adjustments help to shape the personality of the growing boy or girl. If the early environment - including the parents - is excessively frustrating, unresponsive, and distressing, the child will reach adulthood with habitual ways of acting and being that are essentially self-restricting. Indeed, such a person may at some level feel himself or herself to be trapped in a virtual prison of "obsolete responses." This prison, or trap, is the character structure of the individual. Ironically, the very character structure which has been formed as an optimal response to less than satisfactory circumstances comes to represent the most significant obstacle to positive growth and personal development.

The word "character" is derived from Greek and Latin terms meaning "engraving tool" or the mark made by such a tool. The personal development of each individual is engraved in that person's character. To recognize that this is the case is to appreciate the challenging nature of attempting to make significant changes in personal experience and behavior. The individual who has been forced to adjust to distressing circumstances during the early childhood period of dependency will come to view himself or herself - as well as the world at large - through the distorting lens of a restricting characterological attitude. Since the attitude in such a case becomes second nature, any suggestion that an habitual pattern of responses ought to be surrendered will be perceived as threatening. This will be true even if the attitude in question is obviously self-defeating. Perhaps the most striking example of such a dilemma is represented by the individual who is terrified at the prospect of success or pleasure in life. How can such an attitude arise, we may ask, since it seems so contrary to what is natural? The answer is that when faced with a choice between a painful, chronic restriction of oneself and a loss of oneself altogether - as in the case of a threat of overwhelming punishment - children will naturally opt for the former. What appears in the adult to be a fear of pleasure is, in truth, a fear of the pain and anxiety that have come to be associated, through early conditioning, with behavior considered to be unacceptable and dangerous. The most widespread instance of such anxiety-producing behavior in our culture may simply consist of the risk associated with "being oneself."

Under the circumstances, any attempt to re-educate ourselves with respect to a more meaningful and fulfilling way of being must take into consideration certain inner obstacles which impede the establishment of improved functioning. This raises the issue of an inevitable resistance to personal growth and change when such growth and change pose the possibility of genuine characterological transformation.

The word "resistance" may be understood in a variety of ways. In medicine, resistance denotes a positive condition in which the organism has the strength to ward off disease. In the politics of war, resistance refers to the struggle of an indigenous population against an invading army, such as in the case of the French resistance during the Nazi occupation. In the psychoanalytic terminology of Sigmund Freud, resistance signifies a struggle on the part of an individual against allowing painful memories and realizations into consciousness. Interestingly, there are elements of all of these meanings that can be discerned in the resistance to personal growth and change which is rooted in a restrictive character structure. Every individual will resist the anxiety which is associated with effecting a true change of character. This is so because the existing characterological attitude, however restrictive, has provided a genuine resistance to dangers in the past. Carrying on such a resistance to significant change, the individual adopts a posture analogous to the stance taken by resistance fighters attempting to sabotage a hostile force. The rationale for such resistance is to be found in the pain that an individual fears may occur if he or she should act "out of character."

From a functional vantage point, we may say that the character of significant growth and change requires that we recognize and overcome self-defeating resistances. Such a task involves gaining an understanding of the habitual manner in which we organize our self-perception. This is an enterprise involving more than just a change of mind. *Soma* as well as *psyche* is at issue. Layers of resistance are engraved in characteristic ways in the body of the individual. Patterns of muscular tension, limitations in breathing, deficiencies in energy level, and constrictions in the range and quality of movement are all evident in somatic functioning and must be addressed, either directly or indirectly, if real personal growth and transformation are to be promoted.

It is one of the ironies of life that in pursuing serious, constructive alternatives to the limited patterns of action and experience that we have adopted in the interest of self-preservation, we must come face to face with that which we most wish to avoid. In a sense, we must re-experience the original state of conflict which caused us to limit our functioning so that we can resolve the conflict in a satisfactory manner. The conflict between our human need for genuine self-expression and our fear of punishment, for example, must be settled in a mature fashion. Doing so involves dismantling the archaic defenses against rejection and despair that were erected during the helplessness of a childhood endured under adverse circumstances. Indeed, this is the very process which allows us to regain our courage as adults. Paradoxically, it is only by confronting our resistance to change that we can allow change to happen; for in our very resistance is embodied, literally, the energy which must be made available for a more directed, vital, and integrated approach to life. Such an approach to life will necessarily be reflected in increased personal integrity.

The Integrity of the Person

In the world in which we live, most people would probably have little difficulty agreeing that personal integrity has become a rare human quality. The cynic, therefore, is accustomed to argue that integrity is not possible. The idealist is quick to reply that integrity is an abiding virtue. Before deciding whether integrity is an asset or a liability, a practical possibility or a Utopian dream, it might be well to ask what, in fact, the word "integrity" really signifies. If we attempt to view this matter in the flesh-and-blood terms of everyday life, I would suggest that the phenomenon of individual integrity can best be understood as an aspect of the integrated functioning of the person. In this sense, the integrity of the person is a reflection of personal integration. What does this mean?

As human beings, all of us are complex creatures. We are composed of trillions of cells which - with some exceptions, such as the cells of the brain - are continually being born and dying. This body which is mine today is composed, for the most part, of cells which did not exist six months ago. The majority of the cells comprising my living body last Christmas no longer exist. Moreover, the cells of my body have differing shapes and join together to perform different activities. Thus bone tissue does not have the same qualities as cardiac tissue, and the tissue of the heart is distinct from that of the liver or the blood or the skin, the outer layer of which is composed of *dead* cells.

In spite of the great complexity of human beings, however, we normally sense ourselves to be functioning as "simple" organisms. I am myself - not merely a collection of two legs, two arms, a torso, and a head. It is true that a human being can be understood, to a certain degree, as a complex interrelation of parts. Yet the parts of the human organism work together intelligently, each one owing its individual significance to its place in the totality of the person. We can appreciate the importance of keeping in mind the primacy of the organism-as-a-whole if we remember that we all begin as a single, fertilized cell. Differentiation into parts proceeds on the basis of our original unity. In human beings, increasing complexity unfolds out of simplicity. In machines, on the contrary, the whole is constructed by means of an aggregation of pre-formed parts.

Another feature of human complexity is related to the fact that, viewed from the "outside," we are objective beings, while viewed from the "inside" we are subjective in nature. The subjective dimension of life is often called "mind" or "soul." Actually, all of us know both our physical selves and our minds most intimately in a subjective, personal way. My direct awareness of my body is more convincingly real than any textbook account of physiology, and my consciousness of my own experience and behavior is more palpable than any psychological theory. Just as different tissues and organ systems act together to make up our bodies, so the physical and mental sides of our being function together in a unity that embraces our whole selves. In the well-known parable of the blind men encountering the elephant, each person touches only one part of the animal and conjectures about the nature of the beast on the basis of a limited perspective. The elephant, however, is not merely "hard" like its legs or "flexible" like its trunk. In living beings, the diversity of the parts does not provide a sufficient basis for recognizing the true nature of the whole. Body and mind are not separated at the deep level of living functioning.

Based upon these considerations, I think that it is reasonable to suggest that the lack of integrity so characteristic of our current social and cultural milieu is a reflection of a widespread lack of integration in personal functioning. A person who is out of touch with his or her body cannot function with integrity. A person who sees mind and body as radically distinct and separated categories of existence must be at war with his or her own nature. A person whose heart is closed to the sufferings and joys of other people must be an individual who is cut off from the essence of life. To make such assertions is not intended to promote some image of perfect functional integration that is expressed in perfect integrity. Rather, the purpose of these comments is to point out the practical, down-to-earth significance of integrity as more than a beautiful idea or a piece of naive foolishness. A relative degree of integrity - or a relative lack of it - is an inevitable facet of human existence. How much integrity we are able to muster in the face of life's challenges is directly related to the extent of integration in our functioning.

In basic terms, natural human integrity requires that the parts of the person be connected and coordinated in such a way that they act together harmoniously. There are various concrete indices of integrity in human beings. One such index is the degree of comfortable alignment of the various structural segments of the human body in an upright, standing position. As Ida Rolf has consistently emphasized, a quality of easy verticality reflects a proper degree of integration of head, thorax, pelvis, and legs. Similarly, ease and grace of movement reflect the balance and responsiveness of the neuro-muscular system. It must be added that these and other elements of integrated structure and function in human beings are infused with an energetic component. This means that the posture, movement, and personality of the individual can be understood in terms of the flow of feeling, sensation, perception, and emotion. Internal conflict - the psychological counterpart of chronic structural and functional distress - can be comprehended on a bio-energetic level. Personal integrity naturally denotes an absence of habitually blocked motility.

Leaving aside the important issue of prenatal development, let us assume that human beings are born with a relative measure of healthy, integrated functioning. It is not difficult to see that if the basic needs of the infant and child are frustrated or denied the result will be a "dis-integrative" tendency. Under circumstances of deprivation, the integrity of the person will "fall apart." In response, the individual will attempt to hold himself or herself together by force of will. The functional and structural segments of the body must then be bound together by debilitating muscular tensions which serve as a kind of protective armor against disintegration. For human beings, integrity involves basic honesty, rectitude, uprightness, straightforwardness, and adherence to sound principles. The opposite condition involves crookedness, prevarication, and imposture. Words such as these reveal the actual structural and functional basis of human integrity. We need the ability to stand on our own feet, to stand upright, to carry ourselves with a posture that does not force us to straddle the truth (*prevaricate:* to straddle). If we do not have legs to stand on, we will not be able to take a stand on principle. If our backbones are weak, then we will have difficulty backing up our convictions. Seen in this light, personal integrity is a matter of health, which literally refers to the condition of being "whole."

The ultimate solution to the problem of the lack of human integrity is to provide for the true needs of growing children so that they can develop into adults who are capable of being naturally straight, not crooked. Since childrearing methods which would accomplish this purpose are currently rare, a lack of integrity is inevitable. For adults, there exists the challenge of improving personal functioning so that greater integration is effected with respect to the overall life of the individual. This is one manner in which an increase in integrity can become a practical, personal reality. To the extent that such a reality is brought into being, we can be certain that there will be a decrease in the debilitating experience of personal guilt which goes hand in hand with a lack of integrity. Having said this, we can now turn to a consideration of the problem of guilt.

The Problem of Guilt

In legal terms, guilt is adjudged when specific social rules are proved to have been violated in the absence of extenuating circumstances. The personal experience of guilt as a state of being, however, is not so simple to define. Why is it that countless people struggle with a pervasive sense of guilt? Why do so many individuals suffer life as a form of punishment, as a kind of prison sentence to be served until death brings release? Why do others attempt to avoid the problem of guilt altogether by adopting a superficial, "anything goes" philosophy? Is there a connection between an inner sense of unbearable guilt and the devastating and increasingly common violence in our society? In the face of questions such as these, it is reasonable to suspect that an improved understanding of the dynamics of guilt may contribute to a greater sense of personal well-being.

Guilt is related to violence, and in its extreme form it is a contributing factor in the proliferation of anti-social behavior. As Theodore Rubin has pointed out in his book, *Compassion and Self-Hate,* the individual who engages in criminal, harmful behavior and shows no remorse has succeeded in redirecting a violent, intolerable hatred of self onto a sacrificial victim. An extended analysis of the difficult problem which such destructive behavior presents is beyond the scope of the present discussion. We may ask, nonetheless, what is guilt, and how is it related to the struggle for happiness on the part of the average, non-criminal individual who has a chance to grow and make constructive personal change?

At the root of the sense of guilt is aggression turned against oneself. The typical person who feels guilty sees himself or herself as harboring criminal impulses which must be restrained; and indeed, such a person lives in a more or less constant condition of self-imprisonment. It does not matter that a person's sense of guilt may be aroused by actions or intentions which are quite natural - such as asking a member of the opposite sex out for a date, expressing anger toward a spouse, refusing to attend a family gathering, changing jobs, going on a vacation, firing an incompetent employee, sharing a sexual fantasy with ones mate, expressing feelings generally, or simply struggling to get what one wants out of life. What matters to the person who feels guilty is the sense of doom that arises should he or she attempt to break out of the prison of self-confinement. The intensity of this sense of doom can be appreciated if we recognize that the person who suffers from a chronic, underlying feeling of guilt is not only metaphorically, but also *literally* imprisoned. The bars of the prison are composed of the chronically contracted musculature in the body of the "guilty" individual. As Wilhelm Reich has pointed out, these segmental patterns of chronic muscular tension act as a kind of armor and serve the function of restraining impulses of self-expression which are associated with a fear of punishment.

It is interesting that in the German language a single term - *das Schuld* - is used to signify both guilt and debt. Thus the person who has committed a crime is said to be *schuldig* (guilty), just as the person who owes someone money is also designated as *schuldig* (indebted). In my view, it is invariably the case that the person who suffers inappropriately from a sense of guilt is a person who owes a debt, and the debt is inevitably an emotional one. Almost always, as Fritz Perls has suggested, the emotion in question is anger. The anger, however, cannot be released because of the chronic muscular tensions which bind up the aggression of the individual. Such a state of overall muscular tension may keep an individual in bounds and out of trouble, but it also diminishes the person's sense of self, range of

95

movement, choice of behavior, and commitment to life. The result is an habitual feeling of anxiety which is experienced as a form of punishment.

The way out of the trap that such a situation embodies involves gaining a stronger identification with ones true feelings, learning to express oneself emotionally, establishing a commitment to increased honesty with oneself and others, and working to reduce the excessive, habitual muscular tensions that physically anchor the experience of guilt. This does not mean that the solution lies in discharging ones emotions in a thoughtless, careless, self-indulgent manner. Such behavior - quite common in our culture - results from an inability to compose oneself and give direction to ones feelings.

If we are to be honest, we must admit that all of us feel guilty at times, since there are occasions when we betray our own best interests, when we behave inauthentically. On such occasions our feelings of guilt alert us to the fact that we have acted against our principles. Becoming aware of specific behaviors which go against our principles affords us the opportunity to learn from our errors, to make amends, and to deepen our awareness of our true needs and values. The appropriate response in such a situation is to move ahead with our lives in a meaningful direction rather than to engage in self-castigation. The experience of incidental guilt of this kind - "existential guilt," as it has been called - is not to be confused with the chronic tendency toward self-condemnation which retards the genuine development and self-expression of the person.

Why is it that human beings, as a species, are so plagued by guilt, a fact which is reflected in much of the world's mythology and religion, as well as in psychological theory? The answer lies, no doubt, in the human capacity to form value judgments based on mental reflection, an ability which is not shared to a similar extent by any other known animal. In terms of the life of the individual, the seeds of a chronic sense of guilt are sewn in childhood when the person is taught that certain thoughts, feelings, and actions are "bad." The threatened or actual punishments for such offenses serve to mold the character structure of the person and determine the kind and extent of the problems that the person will have in later life in relation to guilt. Sexuality and aggression, which are the main forms of behavior associated with guilt in our culture, are such basic aspects of human experience that most individuals today have learned to feel some degree of guilt about virtually any activity connected with pleasure and self-assertion.

Since chronic guilt entails inner conflicts, the solution to the problem of guilt on a personal level lies in dissolving these conflicts. In terms of the body, the capacity for genuine self-assertion and gratification must be facilitated by raising the energy level of the individual through deepened and expanded respiration. At the same time, habitual restrictions in movement associated with patterns of chronic muscular tension and stress must be reduced. Such positive changes need to be complemented by a sharpened awareness of the determining factors in the childhood situation which are the key to the meaning of the sense of guilt. Enhanced insight, accompanied by genuine changes in somatic functioning, contributes to improved self-understanding. This leads to greater loyalty to self and culminates in the only appropriate verdict for a human being sincerely struggling to meet life's trials: *not guilty*.

Once freed from the bonds of guilt, an individual can make a true commitment to the values and tasks which give life purpose. This is a matter of love, work, and knowledge.

Love, Work, and Knowledge

In his autobiography, the attorney Clarence Darrow writes of feeling little comradeship with either the dreary pessimist or the "cheerful idiot." In fact, a persistent pessimism and an unthinking optimism may be seen to be only partial, exaggerated aspects of a more comprehensive outlook that makes room for both the positive and the negative features of life. To some, such a larger perspective appears unfeasible, for given the difficulties that face human beings in the world and the obvious injustices that can be readily identified, there may appear to be no other alternative than to engage in a "relentless criticism of all existing conditions." Certainly such criticism frequently has merit. Yet no critical venture can prove ultimately to be constructive if it is not supported by a strong commitment to the positive values of life. In this regard, we may be reminded of an observation made by Viktor Frankl in his book, *Man's Search for Meaning.* Frankl, who was imprisoned at Auschwitz during the second world war, remarked that those prisoners who had something awaiting them in the outside world - a loved one, an unfinished task, a responsibility to fulfill - were those most likely to survive the horrors of the concentration camp. For such persons, life held some positive meaning.

It is not my intention in the present context to make judgments or advance proposals concerning the general improvement of the human condition. On a more modest scale, I would simply like to suggest one set of values that can provide an orientation for individual action in the world. Such a set of values cannot be reduced to any rational argument alone, for it stems from a feeling about the meaning of life that is grounded in the experience of living. The positive value of life, I would maintain, is to be found in the realm of love, work, and knowledge. To advance such an idea is to make a positive statement, but it also implies a critical judgment, as will become apparent upon a moment's reflection.

In the course of everyday life, most adult human beings are engaged in the business of earning a living. What such an endeavor entails for each of us varies from individual to individual. In a sense, this is fortunate, since a division of labor in society provides an opportunity for each person to benefit from the concerted application of the unique skills and talents of others. Certainly, in the contemporary world every individual is dependent upon other individuals - either directly or indirectly - for the satisfaction of his or her basic needs. It is also true, however, that the complexity and contradictions which characterize social relationships today have resulted in a set of alienating conditions in which human beings often come to feel themselves to be merely "cogs in a machine." Labor has become so specialized and repetitive that true enjoyment in exercising ones faculties in productive activity is commonly lost. Under such circumstances, what is the value of work?

Closely related to the problem of work is the dilemma of love. We may well ask why love should be considered a dilemma, since at heart most of us recognize that love is the most natural experience in the world. Nonetheless, ample testimony indicates that the authentic experience and the genuine expression of love have fallen prey to the conflicts that divide one person from another, much in the same way that pressures in the struggle for economic survival separate one working individual from another. Just as the cooperation of people employed together at a common task is often tentatively achieved only as a result of short-term expediency, so it is also true that the relationships between members of a family - which on the surface are declared to be based on affection - may at best be only convenient arrangements for attaining a narrow degree of self-interest in a struggle for power. At worst, such relationships may be based on open cruelty and hatred. Inevitably, children raised in families of this kind, in which the experience of love is not a genuine reality, will have difficulties as adults when it comes to loving.

Since it is my proposition that love, work, and knowledge, taken together, may provide a meaningful framework for living, it follows that the *type* of knowledge that we choose to pursue is significant. It is now widely admitted, for example, that advances in the electronic communications field have increased the amount of information in circulation to the extent that many people have become overwhelmed by the sheer mass of details that have proliferated. Yet details - however important in their proper, limited place - are not knowledge. Indeed, genuine knowledge may require that we dispense with some of the sophisticated technical "achievements" that our present state of culture has generated. This is true if knowledge is to fulfill its authentic purpose of furthering the experience of love and promoting the satisfaction that is inseparable from genuinely creative work.

For individuals, the challenge of a meaningful life is bound up with the task of achieving a firm orientation in terms of basic values. Without work, life is impossible. Without love, life is empty. Without knowledge, insecurity is inevitable. The struggle to gain an embodied self-understanding that goes to the roots of life is functionally identical with a commitment to life itself. In order to transform the conditions and circumstances which restrict our existence, we must be mindful of the principles for which we stand. In this regard, I believe that the words of Wilhelm Reich continue to be relevant. "Love, work, and knowledge," he commented, "are the well-springs of our life. They should also govern it." The basic values represented in this outlook are not arbitrarily chosen. Rather, they rest upon the foundation of a deep understanding of the nature of sex, love, and life.

Sex, Love, and Life

Since the period following upon the close of the Victorian era, there has been a significant increase in sexual freedom in the Western world. With that increase in sexual freedom has come the possibility of greater personal fulfillment for many individuals. Has this possibility been realized? In order to answer that question, we must have an adequate understanding of the nature of satisfying sexual functioning. Evidently, such an understanding is not widespread. As Alexander Lowen has pointed out, instead of sexual understanding there exists a prevailing atmosphere of sexual "sophistication."

Perhaps the best example of the sexually "sophisticated" outlook is to be found in the popular saying - "If it feels good, do it!" This outlook can be understood as an expression of rebellion against the strict mores of a sexually repressive, Victorian tradition which emphasized duty and self-control over pleasure and spontaneity. The problem with such an outlook is that it represents a denial of personal responsibility for the consequences of sexual behavior. The attitude expressed in such rebelliousness, moreover, is rigidly determined by the very perspective which it seeks to oppose. As a consequence, the potential for genuine sexual potency is diminished. On a personal level, to assume such a compulsively rebellious sexual posture denotes a condition of being trapped in a set of unresolved conflicts, usually stemming from an unhappy adolescence in which sex was defiantly thought of as "fun." One of the prices paid for such an attitude is the trivialization of a basic biological function; for sex is a fundamental biological fact of life for human beings, and it is only the gratification of sexual needs on a deeply felt biological level that can provide real satisfaction. Yet how are we to understand the biological nature of human sexual functioning?

An answer to this important question has been set forth by Wilhelm Reich in his book, *The Function of the Orgasm.* In that work, as well as in other writings, Reich has pointed out that the smooth functioning of the human organism is dependent upon the accumulation and release of sexual tension. On a deep level, Reich suggests, it is the role of the sexual orgasm to discharge excess biological energy which builds up in the mature individual in the natural course of living. Seen from this vantage point, the orgastic process in human beings represents a basic natural function. Reich has provided the following formula to describe the dynamics of this function: tension → charge → discharge → relaxation. According to this formula, the build-up of organismic tension leads to a state of bio-energetic charge followed by an energetic discharge which culminates in a state of relaxation. The process is governed by a pulsatory rhythm of alternating expansion and contraction. This rhythm can be discerned in all of the basic organismic functions, such as the beating of the heart, intestinal peristalsis, respiration, and the motility of cells. It is Reich's thesis that the dynamic balance - or homeostasis - of the person on a bio-energetic level is orgastically regulated.

That sexual functioning is both a deep and natural occurrence in human beings can be appreciated if due significance is assigned to the phenomenon of biological pulsation. The process of alternating expansion and contraction in a unicellular organism such as the amoeba, for example, leads to a division of the parent organism into two daughter cells. The effect of this process is to relieve accumulated internal pressure within the cellular substance of the amoeba. This is accomplished by the mitotic doubling of the surface area of the amoeba's cellular membrane. In human beings, the reproductive process is more complex, involving specialized sex cells: the sperm and ova. Nonetheless, the orgastic function, which is a natural part of the reproductive process in humans, is a pulsatory phenomenon involving the convulsive discharge of internal pressures in a manner which is functionally identical to that which occurs in the amoeba.

In addition to pulsation, another instance in which biological factors can be seen to lie at the root of sexual attitudes is the evolution of human anatomy, physiology, and social behavior. In the human species, the estrous cycle of the female, with its attendant rutting season, has been replaced by year-round sexual activity. This condition, along with other factors, such as erect posture and increased neurological complexity, have made it inevitable that sexuality must play a central role in the development of human society and culture. This means that, for humans, environmental factors play a significant part in affecting sexual potency.

To be accurate, we must acknowledge that the sexual life of all living organisms is affected to some extent by environmental factors. It is well known, for instance, that experimental animals subjected to excessive stress tend to suffer disturbances in sexual functioning. In laboratory settings, a deprivation of nurturance during the formative period of life can lead to impotence and perversion. It is also true that certain simple organisms in nature - such as the paramecium -

undergo alternating periods of sexual and asexual reproduction, depending on environmental conditions. It should not be surprising, therefore, that human sexual functioning is affected - either positively or negatively - by environmental circumstances. The stage of human sexual maturity, commencing at puberty and continuing at an accelerated rate during adolescence, is a major culminating event in the maturation of the individual. This period marks the transition to adulthood. Inner conflicts which stem from inadequate environmental support during the early childhood years will necessarily impinge adversely on the establishment of mature sexual functioning, just as a lack of support and understanding during puberty and adolescence will undermine sexual security. This is true not only with respect to psychological issues, but also with regard to somatic considerations, especially the existence of patterns of chronic muscular tension. Such patterns of muscular tension represent an attempt on the part of the person to protect himself or herself from pain and anxiety. Unfortunately, armoring of this kind necessarily interferes with organismic motility, with breathing, and with the capacity to surrender to the basic convulsive movements essential to an energetically satisfying orgasm.

Because of the crucial role which the sexual orgasm plays in human functioning, it is important that we neither neglect nor exaggerate the significance of this phenomenon in our attempts to understand the human condition and to bring about improved personal functioning. In bio-energetic terms, sexual functioning in general - and orgastic functioning in particular - are intimately related to breathing, posture, and movement. This is most evident with respect to the inhibitory nature of chronic tensions in the pelvic floor. However, since unimpeded sexual functioning entails the participation of the total organism, it follows that any significant, chronic spasticities and imbalances in the body will be expressed in some degree of disturbance in our ability to surrender to the involuntary sexual movements of orgasm.

Beyond sexual sophistication and sexual repression, there exists the possibility of a more natural, integrated, human sexuality. The increased sense of individuality that characterizes the members of the human species dictates that sexual experience will be most satisfying when it is rooted in a deep awareness of ones own experience and a strong feeling of energetic contact with ones sexual partner. The more of ourselves we bring to the sexual encounter, the more fulfilling the sexual experience will be. It is in this context that the capacity for genuineness of self-expression, depth of affection, and intensity of personal commitment can be translated into an act of surrender to basic biological needs and processes of a sexual nature. For human beings, this means that such an experience is an expression of love. Indeed, for human beings, sex, love, and life - at the deepest level - are functionally identical. To make such a statement is not to deny that human beings have a spiritual nature. On the contrary, it is to provide a potent framework in terms of which the relationship of body, mind, and spirit can be understood.

IV.

Body, Mind, and Spirit

A person's spirituality is not a function of his mind
alone, but of his whole being. The feeling of spirituality,
like any other feeling, is a bodily phenomenon.

Alexander Lowen

Body, Mind, and Spirit

Since all people today belong to the same species, it might seem reasonable to suspect that there would be a general agreement concerning what it means to be human. Even a casual observer, however, cannot fail to realize that no such agreement exists. The confusion and discord characteristic of modern life extend even to the most fundamental questions. Thus, to reflect on the relationship of body, mind, and spirit in human terms poses an interesting dilemma. There are those, for example, who would deny the very existence of the mind, or consciousness, as an actual entity. Others, extolling the virtues of mental awareness, are happy to denounce the spiritual world as an artifact of superstition, fear, and ignorance. Still another group of individuals would like to maintain that the physical world, including the human body, is merely an illusion, a kind of charade which is best transcended. Given the prevalence of such differing viewpoints, it is reasonable to suspect that some degree of conflict regarding these issues is likely to be found not only *among* individuals, but *within* individuals as well. Under the circumstances, it makes sense to attempt to reach some understanding regarding the importance of integrating body, mind, and spirit in the life of the person.

If we begin our consideration of this subject by asking what we mean when we use the term "spirit," we may be surprised to learn that the word actually refers to a bodily process. The Latin root, *spiritus,* literally denotes "breathing." We can see the connection between breathing and spiritual matters reflected in our everyday language in words such as "inspiration" and "aspiration." When we are inspired, we breathe deeply; and when we aspire to some worthy goal, we must breathe fully to supply ourselves with the energy and the spirit to accomplish the task. Even the word "respiration," which means to inhale and exhale air, could also be said to connote, at a deep level, a spiritual function. In living, we constantly renew our spirits in the act of "re-spiration." How are we, then, to understand the connection between the basic bodily processes of breathing and the life of the spirit, which the dictionary defines as "incorporeal" in nature?

Before pursuing this question, we may wish to ask what role the mind plays in our existence. The word "mind" is related to terms such as "mine," "memory," "meaning," and "me." One of the definitions of mind implies that it is an entity that is "opposed to matter," yet clearly the word implies a concrete relationship to the world. The world is reflected in my "mind's eye." I must "re-member" who I am in order to express what is "on my mind," to be "of sound mind," or to "speak my mind." We are all familiar with the way the mind operates - by reasoning, thinking, pondering, and imagining - even if we are not always "of the same mind" with regard to important issues. If we look at the mind as an abstraction, we will necessarily have difficulty determining what substance there is to our mentality. In this case, the natural solution is to remind ourselves of our bodies.

There is another category of experience that belongs in the present discussion. That is the soul, which may be considered to be the realm of our existence which springs from the source of our being. Certainly, soul, spirit, mind, and body are related. Interestingly, the word "soul" is derived from a series of terms which ultimately are related to the word "sea," which may be identified as the original home of human beings. The etymology of the word is instructive, for we know that life on earth has evolved from the sea. The chemical composition of our bodies, which are mostly water, is similar to that of the ocean. The intrauterine environment, too, is much like the sea. In the depths of our souls we are like waves that emanate from pools of feeling. The ability of music to reach us is understandable, in part, in terms of harmonious vibrations which evoke a sympathetic response in our souls. While the soul is thought by some to be immaterial, the word itself refers concretely to actual processes within the self of each person. The soulful quality of a person's existence depends upon the streaming of waves of feeling in the body.

If soul, mind, and spirit all reveal a concrete, even physical significance, as conveyed in the root meanings of the words we use to express these aspects of our experience, it should not come as a surprise to find, in turn, that we cannot reduce the life of the body to the domain of dead matter. Again, this becomes apparent when we attempt to comprehend the meaning of the word "body." Just as there is a tendency to conceive of spirit, mind, and soul as immaterial, there exists a common inclination to designate the body as the mere lifeless, physical structure of a plant or animal. This is the first definition listed in the dictionary. The second definition is that of a corpse or carcass. Surely, however, for human beings what is most important is the *living* body and not a cadaver. The living body is a cauldron of sensation, a brewing, pulsating vat of life. In fact, as Don Johnson has pointed out in his book, *Body,* the word "body" is derived from words meaning "a cask, a brewing tub or a vat." We must distinguish between knowledge we possess *about* the body and knowledge we have *of* the body. The Greeks have given us the name *soma,* which is used to specify the body as a living entity, known to us through the direct, sensuous awareness we have of our corporeal selves. Characteristic of the living body, as distinct from inanimate matter, are sensation and feeling. This means that my body is known to me in an intimate, subjective way. Just as spirit, mind, and soul have a

111

bodily dimension, so the body also has a mental, spiritual, and soulful aspect.

The value of considering the root meanings of words such as "body," "mind," "spirit," and "soul" is that in this way we may gain a deeper insight into the underlying experience which has given birth to these terms. Often, over time, words lose some of their power by being cut off from their roots. Such an occurrence may reflect, in part, a state of alienation on the part of those people who unthinkingly use the words. The suggestion that I am making is that for many people the unitary experience of being alive has become fragmented into diverse and isolated categories. Such fragmentation leads to the mystification of the body, on the one hand, and to the impoverishment of the spirit, on the other.

The fragmentation of body, mind, and spirit is manifested in various characteristic ways. For example, many individuals, in confronting the challenges of living, seek to use their minds to control their bodies. In doing so, they may give lip service to the needs of the spirit. Others attempt to use their minds to *deny* their bodies, retreating into an intellectual fortress of abstract ideas. Still others may flee into a spiritual world in hopes of deriving some sense of protection from the struggles of existence by rejecting the validity of such struggles altogether and by labeling existence an illusion. Another group of individuals succeeds in focusing attention on the body but does so in such a fashion as to make a fetish out of the physical self, which is groomed for specific ends, such as beauty and success. A body which undergoes such an ordeal becomes, as D.H. Lawrence has pointed out, like a "trained dog." Such a body may appear superficially attractive, but it lacks soul and feeling. Inevitably, this lack is clearly reflected in the rigidity, unyieldingness, and artificiality of the person.

If we wish to examine the fragmented quality of much human functioning - as revealed in the everyday behavior of individuals - we will not have to search long for a convenient observation point. We may simply select any shopping mall as our base of exploration. Perhaps the most striking instances of remarkable behavior to be noted in such locales fall under the heading of the way in which parents treat their children. For example, one regularly sees infants in baby carriages and hears their fussing or crying, and yet their parents do not respond. They continue to push the carriage, or they go on talking with a friend. It is as though the crying and fretting of the infant were no more than an electronic signal disturbing the parents' composure, acting as an annoyance which ultimately must, with some reluctance and resentment, be addressed. What the infant needs, however, is immediate responsiveness that leads to an effective resolution of tension. This means that the parents must respond with affection, holding the infant, perhaps changing the diaper and nursing the baby, because this is what the child requires. In order for such requirements to be recognized and accepted, however, the bodies of the parents must be sufficiently alive and "in touch" to sense the meaning of the baby's emotional expressions and to identify with his or her state of being. A lack of responsiveness on the part of the parents toward the child is experienced by the young one as a rejection. The recurrent failure of the parents to respond to the child's needs cannot fail to leave marks on the body, mind, and soul of the immature human being. The irony in this situation is that the parents may have read books on childrearing and may even believe the little one to be a "gift from heaven," a "spiritual child," or a "magical child," as the case may be. Such attitudes, however, only confuse matters in the absence of down-to-earth responses to the child's genuine needs. We cannot influence *soma* without affecting *psyche,* and *vice versa.* Once more, this connection is reflected in our language. *Psyche* means "breath": *psychein* - to breathe, to blow, to live. Where *psyche* (breathing) is concerned, the body *(soma)* is involved.

The advantage of placing a primary focus on the somatic level of human growth and development is that the living body of the person is an objective expression of the person's experience and, therefore, serves as a concrete indication of the state of being of the individual. The expressive movements of the body reveal the spirit and mind. We know this intuitively when we rely on our feelings and sensations as indicators which spontaneously register the meaning of the behavior and attitudes of other people. We understand that the eyes are the "windows of the soul." We sense that the person who holds his or her head naturally high is "spirited." We recognize that the alert person is "bright." Indeed, we say that the exceptionally bright person is "brilliant." Expressions such as these are not simply metaphorical. They refer to the life of the body and to the structure, movement, and energy of the person.

One of the tragedies associated with the estrangement of body, mind, and spirit is that such an estrangement is expressed not only in conflict on an individual level, but in conflict on an interpersonal level as well. This is, perhaps, most evident in the context of the family. Parents, for example, often become angry on account of their children's self-assertion and independence. At the same time, they may find it difficult to accept their children's needs for affection, approval, love, understanding, and respect. Being unable to face their own inadequacies, they may resent and even hate their offspring. In such a situation, the child can be injured without ever being struck. In other instances, children may be physically punished. I was once told of a child who was physically disciplined by a parent for refusing to attend a religious service. After the punishment, the parent forced the child to attend the service and during the ceremony pulled out a handkerchief to wipe away tears inspired by the beautiful sermon. No amount of sentimentality on the part of a parent, however, can compensate for the denial and betrayal of a child on the bodily level.

Just as a denial of the authentic needs of the body produces a spiritual and mental imbalance, so does genuine acceptance of the life of the body create good soil in which real spiritual and mental experiences can take root and grow. Such a statement can be accepted if we realize that body, mind, and spirit are all expressions of the life of the person and are bound together on a functional level. In order to examine and understand this functional level more clearly, it may be helpful to consider the role of energetic factors in the life of the individual.

There are various ways in which we can understand and appreciate the importance of energetic factors in human living. For example, in physiological terms, human beings must assimilate energy from the environment or they will die. Even the most ascetic individual must receive some nourishment, or survival will be forfeited. Simply having enough calories, while a necessary condition to sustain life, is not a sufficient condition to promote it. One must have a minimal amount of emotional contact - including touching - with other human beings, especially during infancy, or one may lose the desire to live. This fact has been elaborated in considerable detail by many authors, including Ashley Montagu in his book, *Touching*. Humans must also discharge energy. A limb that is immobilized indefinitely will wither. Basic impulses and proclivities which are chronically suppressed will find a way to express themselves in distorted fashion and will cause problems. In life, energy is discharged in movement, and the importance of meaningful self-expression in helping to regulate the energy economy of the person is well established. Where there is an integrated, dynamic balance between build-up and discharge of personal energy, there is a degree of harmony in living that is reflected in ones relationship to oneself and to others. This harmony - or lack of it - is manifested concretely in the quality of the expressive movements of the body and the degree of vitality they manifest.

In addressing the issue of improved integration and increased energy in human functioning, a practical approach must necessarily employ a perspective that gives direction and meaning to the process of constructive change and personal growth. Such a perspective is strengthened by taking into account the unity of body, mind, and spirit. We may wish to let go of the restrictions in our functioning that inhibit our pleasure in life, but letting go means surrendering to increased excitation and feeling. Our spirits may be depressed, but until we can improve our breathing, they will not be lifted. For our breathing to improve, chronic tensions in the body must be released. To allow such a process to transpire, we must remember the meaning which our suppressed functions hold for us. The direction of such a venture is toward self-expression which is thoughtful, energetic, spirited, and down-to-earth. The meeting point for these different qualities is the living body. Indeed, both in times of joy and in periods of difficulty, our security is enhanced by reminding ourselves that the life of the body is the ground of our experience.

The Ground of Experience

During periods of personal and social crisis, instability and flux within the environment present a challenge to the individual who wishes to maintain a balanced perspective and a commitment to constructive values. It is at just such times of rapid change and explosive turmoil that personal equilibrium may be difficult to maintain. It is well known that the onset of the Great Depression during the first half of the twentieth century resulted not only in widespread financial hardship but also in psychological despair on the part of many persons. Some individuals awoke as wealthy businessmen on a certain morning only to discover by the time they returned home at sunset that they had been "wiped out." Similarly, critical developments, such as the outbreak of war, may bring much upheaval into the lives of people who are emotionally involved in the unfolding events. If we are to preserve a coherent personal perspective during such tumultuous times, there must exist some base of constancy in our awareness and behavior. In this context, the body may serve as the "ground" of our experience.

To speak of the body as the ground of experience brings to mind the distinction between "figure" and "ground" elaborated in the theory of Gestalt psychology. The dynamics of human perception dictate that some elements in the field of our awareness must stand out as figural in relation to other elements which comprise the background. The whole is composed of both figure and ground. If we wish to maintain contact with the whole of ourselves and avoid a condition of excessive alienation, we must keep in touch with the bodily processes which are at the root of our concerns.

Affirmation of Life

At times when human beings are confronted with sudden change, the normal continuity of life is disrupted, and rapid adjustments must be made. In an attempt to grasp the meaning of circumstances and events, the mind must accelerate its activities in order to comprehend the various implications of unexpected developments. Since major changes affect us in significant ways, it is natural that we make some effort to "take it all in" and to "make sense of it all." In struggling to understand the complexity of our changing reality, we may all too easily find ourselves "up in the air." Yet the very gravity of the situation serves to bring us down to earth. Keeping our feet on the ground becomes both a challenge and a necessity. To meet such a challenge requires that we stay in touch with the life of the body.

The life of the body is more than a mere physico-chemical phenomenon, for the hallmark of embodied living is free-flowing *feeling*, an attribute not reducible to chemicals. As part of their evolutionary heritage, human beings have the capacity for a considerable diversity of emotional expression. The human animal can be hostile as well as compassionate, and acts of loyalty may vie with deeds of treachery in interpersonal relations on a small or large scale. In order for there to be a reasonable and integrated consistency in our responses to life's crises, it is necessary that our experience of somatic reality be anchored in relatively free movements of energy and feeling in the body. The foundation for such relatively open functioning is to be found in the ability to breathe deeply and to tolerate the natural motility of life. Since many events in the modern world provoke considerable anxiety, the preservation and strengthening of a natural process such as uninhibited breathing requires an ongoing commitment to somatic integrity. A commitment of this kind is naturally aided by improving our ability to recognize and understand the underlying structural and functional problems which contribute to destructive conflicts. Making such a commitment may require substantial courage if we live in a mass society in which there is much pressure to conform to destructive modes of behavior.

In an interesting passage in one of his books, Alexander Lowen contrasts the experience of awe with that of horror. He remarks that the sound of jet bombers overhead may be awesome if the bombers are those of ones own military forces flying off to attack the enemy. If one is the enemy, however, the sound of the bombers overhead provokes horror. A related set of contrasting emotions has been elucidated by Karen Horney in her book, *Neurosis and Human Growth*. Horney discusses in some detail the connection between the frequent experience of humiliation in childhood and the search for glory on the part of adults. The quest for glory, in Horney's view, is a defense against inner feelings of inadequacy and insecurity, and it is based on a hatred of ones real self. The desire to be awesome and the struggle for glory, however, are futile endeavors. This is so not because they are morally wrong, but because no substitute can effectively compensate for a lack of genuine fulfillment in life at the bodily level.

Keeping ones feet on the ground means not succumbing to the temptation of power and glory. It also means having the courage to confront the stresses of difficult times with a sense of responsibility and commitment to life. This is a challenge, yet it is life's own challenge and one that cannot be abdicated by human beings without serious consequences. Humiliation, glory, horror, and awe are secondary emotions that may seem to excite or distract us temporarily, but the hard task of sustained living, grounded in an awareness of vital processes within ourselves, is the true challenge of being human. It is also the basis for the affirmation of life.

References

Cousins, Norman. *The Healing Heart* (New York: Avon Books, 1983).

Feldenkrais, Moshe. *The Elusive Obvious* (Cupertino, California: Meta Publications, 1981).

_____ , *The Potent Self* (San Francisco: Harper & Row, 1985).

Frankl, Viktor. *Man's Search for Meaning* (New York: Pocket Books, 1959).

Freud, Sigmund. *Beyond the Pleasure Principle,* trans. J. Strachey (New York: Bantam Books, 1959).

Freudenberger, Herbert. *Burnout: The High Cost of Personal Growth* (New York: Anchor, 1980).

Horney, Karen. *Neurosis and Human Growth* (New York: W.W. Norton & Company, 1950).

Johnson, Don. *Body* (Boston: Beacon Press, 1983).

Kierkegaard, Søren. *Fear and Trembling and The Sickness Unto Death,* trans. W. Lowie (New Jersey: Princeton University Press, 1941).

Laing, R.D. *The Facts of Life* (New York: Ballantine Books, 1976).

Leboyer, Frederick. *Birth Without Violence* (New York: Alfred A. Knopf, 1980).

References

Lowen, Alexander. *Bioenergetics* (New York: Penguin Books, 1975).

_____, *Depression and the Body* (Baltimore: Penguin Books, 1972).

_____, *Narcissism: Denial of the True Self* (New York: Macmillan Publishing Company, 1983).

Montagu, Ashley. *Touching: The Human Significance of the Skin* (New York: Harper & Row, 1971).

Neill, A.S. *Summerhill* (New York: Pocket Books, 1960).

Pines, Ayala, and Aronson, Elliot. *Burnout: From Tedium to Personal Growth* (New York: Macmillan Publishing Company, 1981).

Reich, Wilhelm. *Character Analysis,* 3rd edition, trans. T. Wolfe (New York: Farrar, Straus and Giroux, 1969).

_____, *The Function of the Orgasm,* trans. V. Carfagno (New York: Farrar, Straus and Giroux, 1973).

Rubin, Theodore. *Compassion and Self-Hate* (New York: Ballantine Books, 1975).

_____, *Reconciliations* (New York: The Viking Press, 1980).

Van Gogh, Vincent. *The Complete Letters of Vincent Van Gogh* (Boston: New York Graphic Society, 1978).

Voltaire. *Candide, Zadig and Selected Stories* (New York: The New American Library, 1961).

Index

Index

Index

Index

Ordering Information

The Affirmation of Life can be ordered directly from the publisher. Please enclose $7.95 for each book.

Shipping and Handling: Add $2.00 for the first book and $1.00 for each additional book. (Allow 2-4 weeks for delivery.) For air mail delivery, enclose $3.75 for each book.

International Orders: Enclose $2.50 for the first book and $2.00 for each additional book. (Allow 6-8 weeks for delivery.) For air mail delivery, add $5.00 for the first book and $4.00 for each additional book. Payment must be made in U. S. funds drawn on a U.S. bank.

Ardengrove Press
P.O. Box 219014
Portland, Oregon 97225

About the Author

John Lawson lives with his wife and daughter in Portland, Oregon. Since the early 1980's, he has maintained a practice as a private instructor in Reichian Energetics, a form of personal growth work based on the bio-energetic principles and techniques elaborated by Wilhelm Reich.

In addition to his work with individual clients, Mr. Lawson conducts workshops and seminars, and he lectures frequently on a variety of subjects pertaining to personal growth and improved functioning.